CULTURES OF THE WORLD

ERITREA

Roseline NgCheong-Lum

MARSHALL CAVENDISH
New York • London • Sydney

Reference edition published 2001 by
Marshall Cavendish Corporation
99 White Plains Road
Tarrytown
New York 10591

© Times Media Private Limited 2001

Originated and designed by
Times Books International, an imprint of
Times Media Private Limited, a member of the
Times Publishing Group

Printed in Malaysia

Library of Congress Cataloging-in-Publication Data:

NgCheong-Lum, Roseline, 1962–
    Eritrea / Roseline Ng Cheong-Lum.
      p. cm. — (Cultures of the world)
    Includes bibliographical references and index.
    ISBN 0-7614-1192-5
    1. Eritrea—Juvenile literature.   [1. Eritrea.]   I. Title.
II. Series.

    DT393 .N47 2001
    963.5—dc21

                              00-050834
                                CIP
                                AC

INTRODUCTION

THE YOUNGEST STATE IN AFRICA, Eritrea is also an ancient land where human settlement goes back thousands of years. Situated in northeast Africa, Eritrea is a land of extreme contrasts. The fertile central plateau running down the middle of the country is flanked on both sides by desert lowlands plagued by frequent droughts. Eritrea has one of the lowest and hottest places on earth, Dallol, in the Denakil Depression south of the highlands.

The people of Eritrea belong to several major ethnic groups who trace their origins to as early as before 2,000 B.C. Most Eritreans live in rural areas as peasants and shepherds, scratching a meager living from the unyielding earth.

Having recently emerged from a long war against oppression by neighboring Ethiopia, Eritreans today are channeling their energies into rebuilding their newly independent country. With their freedom, they can look to the future with hope and confidence.

CONTENTS

An Eritrean boy exudes the fresh spirit of freedom in his country.

CONTENTS

The camel is a traditional mode of transportation in rural Eritrea.

GEOGRAPHY

ERITREA LIES ON the northeastern coast of the African continent. Lining the top edge of the Horn of Africa, the country looks like a funnel—wide in the northwest and tapering to a narrow strip in the southeast. With an area of 46,830 square miles (121,320 square km), about the size of Pennsylvania, Eritrea is one of the smallest countries in Africa. Its neighbors are Sudan to the northwest, Ethiopia to the south, and Djibouti to the southeast. Its northeast border runs 715 miles (1,151 km) along the Red Sea, from which Eritrea derives its name (*Mare Erythraeum* is Latin for "Red Sea"). Though blessed with a long coastline and strategic location on an international trade route, Eritrea has always attracted the envy of neighboring nations, especially large and landlocked Ethiopia.

Eritrean territory includes the Dahlak Archipelago—a cluster of 209 islands in the Red Sea that rarely rise above 50 feet (15 m) in height. The country's territorial waters are almost half its land area.

In his book Inside Africa *(1955), John Gunther called Eritrea "a thorny, forlorn splinter of desert-cum-mountain along the Red Sea."*

Left: **Rock and coral in the clear waters of the Dahlak Archipelago.**

Opposite: **A rock pool makes an interesting geographical feature in the rugged terrain of Eritrea.**

THREE REGIONS

Eritrea can be divided into three main sections: the central highlands, the western lowlands, and the coastal plain. These regions differ in terms of terrain, climate, and soil.

The central plateau is a narrow strip of land extending from the Ethiopian Plateau in the south that runs through the middle of Eritrea. The plateau rises to 6,500 feet (1,980 m) above sea level. At its northern end it narrows into a system of eroded hills. Rivers flow through the central highlands, carving deep gorges and small plateaus called *amba* ("AHM-bah").

The central plateau consists of a foundation of crystalline rock covered by sedimentary rock and basalt. The soil is fertile and the climate favorable, which is why agriculture and population are concentrated in this region. Although the central highlands constitute only a quarter of the country's total land area, approximately half of all Eritreans live here. This region includes the Central province and is where the towns of Asmara (the capital of Eritrea) and Keren are located.

The broken and undulating western plain slopes gradually toward the border with Sudan. It lies at an average elevation of 1,500 feet (457 m). The land here consists of sandy soil

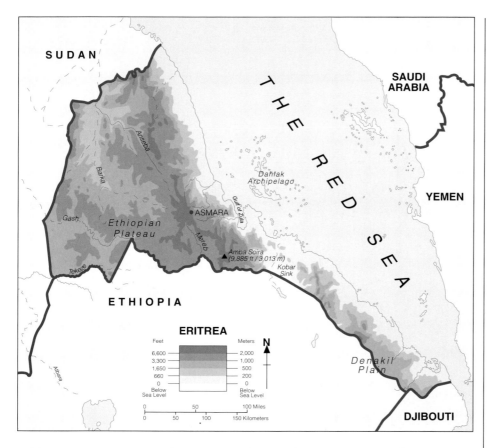

Feet		Meters
6,600		2,000
3,300		1,000
1,650		500
660		200
0		0
Below Sea Level		Below Sea Level

0   50   100 Miles

0   50   100   150 Kilometers

Opposite: **A gorge south of the town of Adi Keyih. Juniper trees grow on the edge of the sandstone-granite escarpment.**

with poor water-retention properties and supports mainly savanna vegetation: scattered trees, shrubs, and grasses.

Eritrea's coastal plain stretches along the Red Sea between the borders with Djibouti and Sudan. It accounts for a third of the country's total land area and encompasses the Northern Red Sea and Southern Red Sea provinces. The coastal plain falls sharply from the central plateau and is narrower in the north—10 to 50 miles wide (16 to 80 km)—than in the south, where it widens to include the Denakil Plain. This barren region is part of the Denakil Depression, which Eritrea shares with Ethiopia. The coastal plain is part of the East African Rift System, a deep valley running from Tanzania in the south to the Red Sea, that was created some 25 million years ago by the collision of tectonic plates. The coastal plain suffers from poor soil quality and supports little vegetation. The main towns in this region are the port cities of Massawa and Assab.

THE DAHLAK ISLANDS

Eritrea's Red Sea region contains 354 islands and islets, of which only ten are inhabited. Some 209 islands lying off the shore opposite Massawa make up the Dahlak Archipelago. The largest island is Dahlak Kebir with an area of 248 square miles (643 square km). It is home to 60% of the archipelago's 2,500 inhabitants, mainly fishermen and cattle herders.

The Dahlak Archipelago has been designated a national park to preserve its teeming marine life, which includes dolphins, sharks, dugongs, turtles, hermit crabs, and seashells. Mangroves, shoals, coral reefs, and pumice stone formed from underwater volcanoes rank among its other interesting features.

Below: **Mangrove trees arch over a swamp near the coastal town of Tio.**

Opposite: **A mountain towers over trees and passers-by.**

The government is attempting to develop the Dahlak Islands into tourist resorts to attract diving and beach enthusiasts while protecting the natural marine resources, one of Eritrea's most important assets. The Red Sea's saline warm waters are a colorful haven for more than 1,000 species of fish and coral.

MOUNTAINS AND RIVERS

Eritrean terrain is mountainous with tremendous topographical variation. The highest point in the country is Amba Soira, one of several mountains in the highlands. It rises to a height of 9,885 feet (3,012 m). The lowest point, 381 feet (116 m) below sea level, is inside the Kobar Sink in the Denakil Plain.

Four major rivers and numerous streams drain the central highlands, but only a few seasonal streams flow all the way to the Red Sea. The Barka and Anseba rivers flow north to the east coast of Sudan but stop short of reaching the Red Sea. The Gash and Tekeze rivers form parts of Eritrea's border with Ethiopia as they flow west into Sudan. The Tekeze is a tributary of the Atbara River, which later joins the Nile. The Gash crosses the western lowlands, and its upper course, known as the Mereb, flows along the border on the plateau.

A boy draws water from a hole in a dried-up river bed.

CLIMATE

The altitude differences in Eritrea produce extreme variations in climate. The central plateau experiences a moderate climate with highs of 86°F (30°C) in May and near freezing lows in December through February. In the western lowlands the hottest months of April, May, and June reach 106°F (41°C), while the coolest month is December when temperatures average 55°F (13°C). On the coastal plain winter temperatures range between 70°F (21°C) and 95°F (35°C), while summer from June to September sees temperatures rising as high as 122°F (50°C). The Denakil Depression is the hottest place in the country.

There are two rainy seasons. The "short rains" fall in March and April; the main rains last from late June to early September. The central plateau experiences the most rain, with an annual average of 16 to 20 inches (406 to 508 mm). The western lowlands receive less than 16 inches (406 mm) a year, while the coastal plain is far drier. The inner parts of the Denakil Plain are virtually rainless.

HOT SPOT

Sprawling across the Eritrean-Ethiopian border near Djibouti, the Denakil Plain in the Denakil Depression is one of the most inhospitable places on earth. This dramatic landscape of deserts, rocks, salt formations, and black volcano cones is one of the lowest places on earth not covered by water. It reaches a maximum depth of 380 feet (116 m) below sea level inside the Kobar Sink. The plain boasts the world's hottest place as well: the town of Dallol experiences an annual mean temperature of 94°F (34°C). The blistering sun and strong winds make survival here impossible for most plants and animals. However, such harsh conditions have not kept commercial enterprises from exploiting mineral deposits in the depression. As early as 1912, the Italians built a railway to the region to transport potash mined in Dallol to the coast.

The little village of Badda serves as a gateway to the Denakil Depression. The fertile land here supports the cultivation of crops. Sunday markets attract camel caravans across the moon-like Denakil Plain, although sandstorms, which strike between 1 and 4 PM everyday, reduce visibility to less than 33 feet (10 m). The village's main attraction, however, is the turquoise Lake Badda (pictured below). It sits in an ancient volcano crater some 1,313 feet (400 m) wide and 328 feet (100 m) deep.

The Denakil Depression has attracted recent international interest as the site of the discovery of a one-million-year-old skull. The well-preserved fossil shows characteristics of both *Homo sapiens* and *Homo erectus* (the ancestor of modern humans), providing yet another link in the evolution of the human race.

FLORA AND FAUNA

Thirty years of war and recurrent drought have taken a heavy toll on Eritrea's natural world. The massive destruction of forests, accompanied by illegal hunting, has resulted in the near extinction of many plant and animal species. The government has undertaken strict measures in the last decade to restore the country's ecological environment. Captive breeding, land reservation, reforestation, and public awareness campaigns are still being carried out with considerable success, and the country's formerly abundant flora and fauna seem to be on the road to recovery.

Trees and other plants growing in Eritrea include baobab, pine, eucalyptus, olive, aloe, and sisal. Some, like the ficus, are on the endangered list. The area around Rora Habeb, a plateau southwest of the town of Nakfa in the Northern Red Sea region, has one of the last juniper forests in the country. Vegetation here survives on nocturnal condensation rather than rainfall. Shrubs and grasses associated with the savanna green the landscape of the western lowlands. Tropical flowering plants, especially acacia, bougainvillea, and jacaranda beautify all the major towns.

Efforts to preserve the country's animal

diversity are resulting in the return of elephants, leopards, rhinoceroses, gazelles, antelopes, wild hogs and donkeys, hyenas, and ostriches. Smaller animals making a comeback include rabbits, rodents, and monkeys. There are also the fish and birds of the Red Sea islands. More than 100 bird species feed on sardines and anchovies migrating through the Red Sea. Sheep, goats, cattle, and domesticated camels are raised by farmers and shepherds. The camel has been adopted as the national emblem for its instrumental role in transporting supplies during the war for independence.

Locusts are a pest in Eritrea. They compete with humans for food as they attack a wide range of crops and trees and can eat their own weight in food everyday.

Below: **Locusts devouring a small plant.**

Opposite: **The aloe is one of the many and diverse plant species in Eritrea.**

ASMARA

Perched one and a half miles (2.4 km) high on the central plateau, Asmara became the capital of Eritrea in 1897 when the Italian colonial authorities decided to shift their administrative center here, away from the sweltering heat of the coastal town of Massawa. With a population of about 400,000 today, Asmara is the largest city in the country.

The name Asmara comes from *arbate asmara*, which means "they united the four." According to legend, when fighting broke out among four small villages in the region, the village women collaborated to unite their people. Another legend says the Queen of Sheba bore King Solomon a son in this region.

Unlike most capital cities on the African continent, Asmara is safe enough for residents and tourists to roam the streets both day and night. The city features a large central market selling vegetables, spices, clothing,

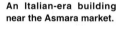

An Italian-era building near the Asmara market.

baskets, and pottery among other items. But the heart of the city is Liberation Avenue, where cafés and bars abound, as do bougainvillea and jacarandas. In the evenings residents promenade along the avenue, sip coffee in the cafés, and shop in the stores.

Much of the city was built in the 1920s and 1930s. There are some tall buildings in the city center, but most houses, like the old Italian villas, are one or two stories high. Asmara was defended by Ethiopian troops during the war for independence and so escaped the devastation sustained by towns like Massawa and Keren. One of the oldest and most beautiful buildings in Asmara is the former Imperial Palace, built in 1897. It is now the National Museum. Among Asmara's many important buildings and places are the Supreme Court, the City Hall, the National Bank, the Asmara Theater, the Asmara University, the Catholic Cathedral, the Khulafa el-Rashidin Mosque, and the Inda Mariam Orthodox Church.

Cars and buses travel up and down the scenic Liberation Avenue.

17

A mat seller at a market in Keren.

OTHER MAJOR TOWNS

Keren is the most important highland town after the capital Asmara. Nestled amid mountains, Keren, which means "highland," sits 4,567 feet (1,391 m) up on a plateau and enjoys a temperate climate. It has a large Muslim population and many mosques. The lively market here attracts traders from the region, who haggle over camels, donkeys, and sheep. Keren was severely damaged in the country's struggle for independence.

Massawa and Assab are modern and prosperous port cities. Massawa is the country's main port and its second largest city. It is also the largest natural deepwater port on the Red Sea coast. Causeways link the mainland part of Massawa to two islands, Batsa and Twalet. The port itself is on the island of Batsa. Because of Massawa's strategic coastal location, it has always been an important trading center. It too suffered heavy shelling by the Ethiopians during the war for independence and is being rebuilt. Blessed with some good beaches, Massawa is a popular weekend destination for many families.

Few buildings in Massawa survived the war of independence undamaged.

18

Assab thrives mainly because it is the nearest port for Ethiopian traders. When Eritrea finally freed itself from Ethiopian domination in 1991, the government guaranteed Ethiopian traders a safe route to Assab. The port combines industry and leisure, boasting clean spacious beaches, while producing salt for both domestic use and export.

Nakfa is special in every Eritrean's heart, for it was from here that liberation fighters launched their offensive against Ethiopian forces in the 1970s. The new currency was named after Nakfa in 1997 to commemorate the significance of the town in the country's history.

Eritrea's smaller towns include Agordat in the western lowlands, Tio and Ed on the coast, and Teseney close to the border with Sudan.

The ruins of the former Banco di Roma in the port district of Massawa.

HISTORY

THE DISCOVERY in Eritrea of one of the oldest human fossils ever found hints at the length of human existence in the country. Eritrea may well be the cradle of our species. The first people to settle in the area came from the region of the Nile. These Nilotes occupied the northern parts of Eritrea. Later migrants from the ancient North African kingdom of Cush inhabited the Eritrean highlands. By 1,000 B.C. or earlier, Semites crossed the Red Sea from the South Arabian kingdom of Sheba and invaded the lands of the Cushitic settlers. The Semitic occupants introduced the ancient Ge'ez script, the root of the languages used in Eritrea today. They also brought camels and sheep and developed irrigation schemes and hillslope terraces, thus laying Eritrea's agricultural foundations and setting the stage for the reign of the Axumites, the first of many "outsiders" to rule Eritrea for the next three millennia before its independence.

In the 16th century Eritrea was known as Medr Bahr *(Land of the Sea).*

Left: **A grave holds the remains of an Eritrean tribe's ancestors.**

Opposite: **Archeological sites in Eritrea remind present-day generations of their ancient past.**

Above: **The stele of Ezana bears records of Axumite wars in Eritrea. Axumite reign saw the evolution of a distinct architectural style.**

Opposite: **A Turkish-style window on the Administration Building in Keren is a remnant of Turkish rule in Eritrea.**

THE KINGDOM OF AXUM

The kingdom of Axum rose to prominence in the fourth century A.D. and peaked in prestige in the seventh century. It stretched from Nubia (now Syria) into southern Arabia (now Yemen), then across the Red Sea into Somalia. Its capital city was in Ethiopia, but it had important towns in Eritrea as well. Axum controlled the land and sea routes from Africa to Europe and Asia and monopolized trade in the region. Its principal port, Adulis, was a trading center for gold, gems, incense, and other goods.

The Axumites are known for several achievements during their reign in Eritrea. One king, Ezana, is believed to have introduced Christianity to the region. Victory over the Jewish king of Yemen, who persecuted Christians, and the arrival of Syrian missionaries, who contributed significantly to the Church, earned Axum great prestige and consolidated its position as a powerful defender of the Church. But Adulis was destroyed in A.D. 710, and for the next few centuries Ethiopian dynasties and Muslim sultanates battled for power in Eritrea.

THE TURKO-EGYPTIAN ERA

The Ottoman Turks entered Eritrean history in the 16th century, amid a backdrop of feuding kingdoms in the region. They occupied the Eritrean coast in 1517 and took control of Massawa. However, the Portuguese and Abyssinians combined forces to wrest Massawa from them in 1543. Control of the town then alternated between the Turks and these opposing forces until 1562. The Turkish leader then ruled most of Eritrea for 15 years with the Abyssinian emperor, until the latter beheaded him. What followed was another tug-of-war between the Turks and the Abyssinians. Finally, in 1589 the Turks agreed to a peace deal with the Abyssinians and remained as a power in Eritrea for another three centuries.

The Egyptians were a threat in the region in the middle of the 19th century. They invaded Sudan in 1820 and penetrated Ethiopia in 1840. In 1846 they stepped onto Eritrean shores by signing a lcasc for Massawa. By 1853 they had conquered the western lowlands and the area around Keren, and by 1875 they had occupied more territory on the coast. However, Egyptian power in the region faded as Egypt came under the British protectorate in the 1880s. The European chapter had begun.

Above: **The Abyssinian emperor was persuaded to release his Italian prisoners. The Battle of Adua was one of the biggest battles in Africa.**

Opposite: **The British war cemetery on the edge of the town of Keren testifies to a major battle in 1941, in which the British defeated the Italians.**

ITALIAN COLONY

The Italians came to Africa after the French and the British had secured their presence in the region. They established their administration in Assab in 1882 and ousted the Egyptians from Massawa in 1885. A few years later they raised their flag in Keren and Asmara. By 1889 the Italians held most of Eritrean land, and the next year they proclaimed the territory an Italian colony and officially named it Eritrea. Desiring Ethiopia, they clashed with the Abyssinians at Adua in 1896. The latter became the first African power to defeat a European army. The two sides later signed a treaty recognizing Italian rule over Eritrea. In 1898 Signor Martini became Eritrea's first civilian governor, and by 1910 the colony's provincial structure was in place.

The Italians built railroads, ports, plantations, and factories, and introduced modern ways of living in their colony. Eritrea soon overtook Ethiopia in material progress. By 1929 Massawa was the biggest port on the east coast of Africa, and by 1937 Eritrea was the center of a regional transport network employing some 100,000 people.

BRITISH PROTECTORATE

In 1935 the Italians launched their planned attack on Ethiopia from their Eritrean base. Six years later, the British returned and forced them back into Eritrea. The Italians lost several towns in a matter of months. Their surrender of Asmara on April 1, 1941, sealed their defeat in Eritrea, which now faced a new master.

The British were unprepared to run a new administration and so made few (though substantial) changes to the existing one. They retained the Italian officials, but lifted the color bar and trained Eritreans in civil service and education.

The British continued to invest only while Eritrea remained useful to their North Africa strategy. Toward the end of World War II, in 1944, they began removing infrastructure, equipment, and remaining supplies. Eritrea's economy collapsed in 1946, plunging the country into a state of social unrest.

During the crisis, Ethiopia intended to annex Eritrea, while the British proposed to partition the country between Sudan and Ethiopia. Eritrea's future was debated internationally until 1952, when the British protectorate years ended with a UN resolution to grant it autonomy within a federation with Ethiopia.

FEDERATION

To find out what the Eritreans themselves wanted for their future, the United Nations sent a fact-finding mission to Eritrea. However, the Commission of Enquiry, fed with misinformation by the British, reported on June 28, 1949, that the Christian majority in Eritrea were in favor of union with Ethiopia.

On December 2, 1950, the United Nations passed a resolution to federate Eritrea with Ethiopia. Similar to the relationship between the US states and the federal government, Eritrea would be an autonomous unit governing itself under the sovereignty of Ethiopia. The federal scheme took effect on September 11, 1952.

However, the Ethiopian emperor, Haile Selassie, soon began to violate the act of federation. He increasingly interfered in the federal government's administration, banning Eritrean political parties and trade unions and replacing the major languages of Tigrinya and Arabic with Amharic, Ethiopia's official language. Within a decade, the Selassie regime systematically annexed Eritrea, overwhelming its federal government and imposing its own law in the federation.

The federation of Eritrea with Ethiopia was not enough to satisfy Emperor Haile Selassie's thirst for power.

Eritrea lost its federal status for good in 1962, becoming Ethiopia's 14th province. But the angry Eritrean people had no way to fight back. Protesters suffered at the hands of the police and were jailed or forced into exile. Getting outside help was impossible, as their head of state was Selassie's own son-in-law. The only solution seemed to be armed struggle, a reality Eritrea would face for the next 30 years.

FIGHT FOR FREEDOM

The Ethiopian regime in Eritrea razed villages, kidnapped and killed innocent people, jailed or exiled political leaders, drained economic resources, and displaced hundreds of thousands of people, many of whom sought refuge in neighboring Sudan.

In 1960 exiled Eritreans in Cairo formed the Eritrean Liberation Front (ELF) to raise arms against the Ethiopians. The ELF received enthusiastic support from disgruntled Eritrean workers and students, and soon the revolution spread to the central highlands in Eritrea. However, internal disagreements caused some members to defect and form another movement, which would later be named the Eritrean People's Liberation Front (EPLF).

Although the two fronts continued to fight each other—even when Selassie was overthrown in Ethiopia in 1974 and replaced by a new military dictator—they succeeded in freeing most of the Eritrean towns from Ethiopian grip. In fact, they might have won control of Eritrea, if not for the delivery of new armaments to Ethiopia in 1977 by the Soviet Union. Within a year, the Ethiopian regime had regained most of Eritrea, and the ELF and the EPLF were forced to retreat and start again. Only the EPLF survived, fed by a steady flow of Eritreans eager to fight for their freedom. The EPLF, as the champion of Eritrean nationalism, fought the bloody war against Ethiopia for another decade, reclaiming Eritrea town by town. When the Soviet Union withdrew its military aid to Ethiopia in the late 1980s, Ethiopia fell. In May 1991 the EPLF assumed complete control of Eritrea.

The cruel liberation war has left a permanent scar on the Eritrean psyche.

THE ERITREAN PEOPLE'S LIBERATION FRONT

The first group to form against Ethiopian rule was the Eritrean Liberation Movement (ELM). Founded by young Eritreans exiled in Sudan, it attracted both Muslim and Christian Eritreans. With no clear plan, the ELM had a short life. In July 1960 exiled Eritreans in Egypt set up the Eritrean Liberation Front (ELF). This Muslim-dominated movement soon became the leader of the war against Ethiopian rule. To enable Christian Eritreans to join the armed struggle, the People's Liberation Front (PLF) was formed in 1971. A year later, the Eritrean Liberation Force (another ELF) formed and merged with the PLF. The ELF-PLF coalition later became the Eritrean People's Liberation Front (EPLF), which took several towns back from the Ethiopians. The ELF had its fair share of military victories, but it withdrew in 1980, leaving the EPLF to fight the war alone. The EPLF fought unceasingly for another decade, emerging victorious in Asmara in 1991. The greatness of the EPLF was not just its military success, but also its farsighted preparation of the population for independence. While training youths in warfare (pictured above), EPLF leaders also taught them the banned Tigrinya language to preserve their heritage. Many Eritreans received their education this way. After independence the EPLF became the People's Front for Democracy and Justice (PFDJ), from which most of today's Eritrean leaders come.

INDEPENDENCE

When the residents of Asmara realized that the city had been liberated at 10 AM on May 24, 1991, they ran out of their houses and danced in the streets. For the first time in over a hundred years, they were free.

The EPLF established a provisional government and held a national referendum in April 1993 to conclude the country's struggle for freedom. Almost everyone who voted chose independence, and on May 24, 1993, Eritrea was formally declared independent. Relations with Ethiopia started out smoothly, owing to the close friendship between the new Eritrean and Ethiopian leaders. As a gesture of goodwill, Eritrea guaranteed Ethiopian access to the Red Sea through the port of Assab.

In 1997, however, relations between the two neighbors soured when Ethiopia drew up a new map that placed parts of southwest Eritrea in Ethiopian territory. Fighting broke out as each side tried to capture the disputed land. A truce brokered by US and Italian mediators halted the fighting at the end of 1998, but a few months later the two sides clashed again, and no solution has been reached so far.

Eritreans celebrating their country's independence. Of the 98.5% of eligible voters who cast their ballots in the national referendum in April 1993, 99.8% said "yes" to independence.

GOVERNMENT

THE NEWEST STATE IN AFRICA, Hagere Ertra (State of Eritrea) was proclaimed on May 24, 1993. To reflect the changed political conditions, the provisional government set up after liberation was reorganized into the People's Front for Democracy and Justice (PFDJ). The PFDJ, now the only legitimate political party in the country, participates in the legislative branch of the democratic government of Eritrea. Known as the National Assembly, the legislature elects the president.

Eritrea's first and current president is Isaias Afwerki, who led the EPLF in its fight for independence. He and his cabinet of 16 ministers head the executive branch—the State Council—of the government. The State Council includes regional governors and other officials, who aid the cabinet in implementing the policies and laws of the government. The judiciary consists of courts at national, regional, district, and village levels.

Isaias Afwerki won 95% of the National Assembly vote on June 8, 1993. As president, he is the head of the government and can serve a maximum of two five-year terms.

Left: **The City Administration Building in Keren.**

Opposite: **The flag of independent Eritrea.**

31

The Eritrean people have yet to exercise their right to vote in a national election. The outbreak of the border conflict with Ethiopia has delayed the holding of the first countrywide election.

Voting is a new experience for this young nation.

THE LEGISLATURE

The National Assembly outlines the domestic and foreign policies of the government, regulates the State Council's execution of these policies, approves the country's budget, and elects the president. It also ratifies the president's nominations of leaders for the various ministries, authorities, commissions, and offices.

Of the 150 seats in the legislature, 20 have been reserved for women to encourage female participation in governing the country. The PFDJ's Central Committee makes up half of the total membership, while the other half consists of representatives directly elected by the general population. Sixty of the latter come from the Constituent Assembly, which was set up to ratify the country's first constitution. The remaining 15 elected members represent Eritreans living abroad. Local and regional elections were held in 1992 and 1997 respectively.

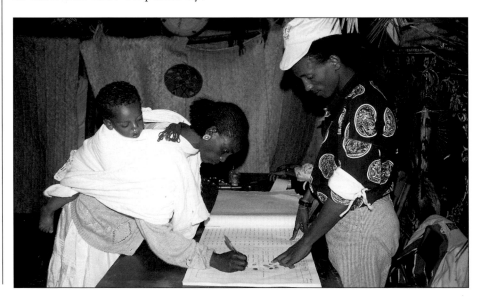

THE CONSTITUTION

After independence in 1993, the government set up a Constitutional Commission to draft Eritrea's first constitution. To ensure the best constitution possible, the commission sought the views of as many Eritreans as possible, both at home and abroad. Even Eritrean refugees in Sudan were involved in the information-gathering process. The constitution was promulgated in May 1997.

The country's democratic constitution guarantees freedom of expression and equal rights for all Eritreans, regardless of gender, race, or religion. It also authorizes a multiparty system and allows any number of political parties to take part in elections, provided they are not based on religious or ethnic foundations.

Eritreans age 18 and above are entitled to vote in both regional and national elections. However, presidential and parliamentary elections due in 1998 were postponed indefinitely due to the outbreak of the border conflict with Ethiopia.

Refugees returning from Sudan. The views of these displaced Eritreans counted in the drafting of their country's first constitution.

The Eritrean Liberation Front (ELF) is now a political pressure group in the democratic State of Eritrea.

THE JUDICIARY

The judiciary is independent of the legislative and executive arms of the government. The Ministry of Justice oversees a three-tier legal structure—the high court, regional courts, and subregional courts—that administers justice from the national level down to the villages.

The highest court is the Supreme Court, established in the constitution. The top judges are appointed by the president. Next come the city courts, which administer justice in the large cities. At the regional level, there are ten provincial courts and 29 district courts. Special Sharia courts cater to the Muslim population, following Islamic Sharia law in family cases.

Reliance on the Ministry of Justice for logistical and financial support has hampered the judiciary's independence. It is subject to executive interference, due to poor funding and the lack of trained staff.

INTERNAL ADMINISTRATION

Eritrea is divided into six regions, each of which has its own capital. Asmara is the capital city of both the central province and the entire country. Each region is further divided into subregions and towns.

Regional governors are nominated by the president and their appointment ratified by the National Assembly. A governor oversees a team of local councilors, who are directly elected by the residents of their village or town. Regional elections held in 1997 chose 399 representatives for the Constituent Assembly. In local elections in 1992, 12,000 candidates made it to the local councils. Each council manages the daily running of a constituency and looks after the welfare of the residents.

Regional and local administration is often inefficient due to a lack of qualified staff. Jobs in this arena are new to Eritreans, who have only recently assumed control of their nation.

NATIONAL SYMBOLS

The Eritrean flag is split into three triangles. Starting from the hoist edge, a horizontal red isosceles triangle divides the rest of the flag into two right triangles, the upper one green and the lower one blue. A gold olive wreath is superimposed on the red section. The national flag is a combination of two other flags: the old Eritrean flag and the EPLF flag (both pictured below). The national flag draws the laurel-olive symbol from its 1952–59 predecessor and the colored triangles from the EPLF flag. The president's flag is similar to the new national flag, but with the country's national emblem in the place of the olive wreath. The national emblem is a camel encircled by an olive wreath.

The Eritrean currency is a national symbol in itself, having been named after the town of Nakfa, the location of the launch of the country's armed struggle against the Ethiopian regime.

A place that is set to become a potent national symbol is the National Martyrs' Park. Dedicated on June 19, 1997, the eve of Martyrs' Day, it boasts more than 692 acres (280 hectares) of beautiful plains, valleys, and mountains in the highlands just southeast of Asmara. The Eritrean government views the park as the most important historical and natural resource to be passed from one generation to the next. Each tree in the park commemorates one of the 65,000 fighters and tens of thousands of civilians who lost their lives during the fight for freedom from Ethiopian rule. The park is a national enterprise. Every Eritrean, whether in the country or abroad, is adopting a tree. The park also features the National Martyrs' Monument, on which each martyr's name is engraved, and museums detailing the country's fight for independence.

Eritrean troops celebrate after retaking the town of Teseney from Ethiopian forces on June 6, 2000.

In 1998, 120,000 National Service reservists were activated to supplement the 47,100-strong armed forces. More have been deployed since, inflating the combined armed forces to 200,000.

NATIONAL SERVICE

Every Eritrean between the ages of 18 and 40, male or female, has to contribute to the country's welfare by performing two years of national service. Students who have completed secondary school spend one month repairing roads or helping to educate illiterate adults. National service teams have constructed dams and wells, repaired roads, terraced hillsides to reduce erosion, and planted millions of tree seedlings.

Men between the ages of 18 and 40 serve in the military for six months at a place called Sawa. Eritrea has a big military sector, which includes an air force. The largest part of the military is the army, despite government efforts to demobilize the EPLF force. Eritrean troops are concentrated near the borders with Sudan and Ethiopia. The small navy protects the country's Red Sea coast and islands. Defense expenditures took up nearly 30% of the gross domestic product (GDP) in 1997. This is a substantial amount for one of the world's poorest countries, though perhaps justified by recent hostilities with its neighbors.

INTERNATIONAL RELATIONS

Eritrea is a member of a number of international organizations, including the United Nations, the World Health Organization, the International Monetary Fund, the Organization for African Unity, and the African, Caribbean, and Pacific group of Third World countries that get preferential access to certain European Union markets. Eritrea also maintains friendly relations with several European countries—especially its former colonial master, Italy—and with the United States.

Relations with the immediate neighbors, however, are not as healthy, mainly because of territorial disputes. Competition with Yemen over the Hanish Islands in the Red Sea was resolved with international arbitration in 1998.

Eritrean President Isaias Afwerki *(right)* **walks with Algerian President Abdelaziz Bouteflika at Asmara airport on May 25, 2000.**

Also in 1998 the border conflict with Ethiopia flared into a war, which persists today, destroying buildings and killing civilians, adding to the ruins of past wars. Relations with Sudan, where many Eritrean refugees still await repatriation, have chilled as the Eritrean government has grown wary of the Islamic fundamentalist system prevailing in its northern neighbor.

Although Eritrea is in dire need of economic aid, the government practices great caution in accepting any form of help from other countries. It will flatly refuse offers that come with strings attached—unreasonable conditions that may endanger the young and fragile country's freedom. Neither does it favor aid from international nongovernmental organizations such as the Red Cross. Instead, Eritreans remain steadfast in their desire to own their land, working proudly to become self-reliant and to build their country on their own.

ECONOMY

WHEN THE EPLF LIBERATED ERITREA in 1991, they faced a devastated country. The ravages of war were worsened by droughts and famines, which followed soon after. The only thing the country had going for it was the absence of external debt, a burden that Ethiopia had agreed to bear. Today, foreign exchange for the Eritrean economy comes mainly from annual remittances totaling an estimated US$75 million sent by its citizens living abroad.

Despite the odds, the government remains determined to achieve economic self-sufficiency for its people. It welcomes foreign investment on the sole condition that this poses no threat to the country's hard-won freedom. This economic strategy seems to be working: Eritrea has seen steady growth since independence and estimates that its gross domestic product (GDP) will grow by 6.2% in 2000.

In Eritrea, one of the world's poorest nations, each person lives on an average annual income of US$210. This is less than half the figure for sub-Saharan Africa. Two-thirds of the population depend on food aid.

Left: **Port machinery in operation at the port in Assab. Port activities contribute around half of the country's GDP.**

Opposite: **A woman explores items for sale at a colorful market.**

AGRICULTURE AND PASTORALISM

Nearly 80% of the Eritrean population depend on agriculture for a living, and agricultural products make up the bulk of the country's exports. Despite poor soils, unreliable rainfall, and archaic cultivation methods, agriculture accounts for a significant 15% to 25% of GDP. Yet this still fails to meet domestic needs. A bumper crop in 1992 satisfied only 42% of overall demand. Nevertheless, there is great potential for improvement. Of the 8 million acres (3.2 million hectares) of arable land in the country, only 5% is cultivated. Soil erosion on the central plateau and severely depleted forest resources also present major challenges to the industry.

Before World War II, the Italian colonists set up large irrigated plantations producing a variety of cash crops, but the war destroyed almost everything, and cultivation is now done mostly by subsistence farmers. These farmers produce food for their own use and a small surplus for trade.

Eritrea needs from 600,000 to one million metric tons of grain annually to feed its population. In good years, it meets nearly 25% of this demand, importing the rest from Ethiopia. The country has recently turned to the United States and Europe for wheat and sorghum.

Peasants gather the harvest in a teff field near the town of Senafe.

A shepherd herds his flock of goats down a road in Keren.

Farmers in the highlands grow several types of traditional grain, such as teff, wheat, millet, barley, and corn. Teff looks like millet and contains yeast, which makes it rise. High in protein, complex carbohydrates, and minerals and low in fat, teff is an ideal food and is used to make the national staple *injera* ("in-JEHR-uh"). The main crops on the lowlands are sorghum, millet, and corn, though this region also supports the growing of vegetables and tropical fruits, like papayas, bananas, and oranges. Plantations on the escarpment produce cotton, sesame, coffee, rubber, and tobacco.

Closely related to agriculture is pastoralism, another traditional Eritrean occupation. Pastoralists earn their living from animal husbandry, rearing goats, camels, sheep, and cattle for milk and meat. Some tribes, like the nomadic Beja and Afar, consist mostly of shepherds, who wander through the lowlands with their herds according to weather conditions. Agriculturalists, on the other hand, settle in the highlands, but the two occupations are not mutually exclusive: farmers may rear some animals, and shepherds may cultivate some grain.

41

FISHING

With a long coastline and large territorial waters, fishing holds long-term prospects for the Eritrean economy. Species for exploitation include tuna, cuttlefish, crabs, parrotfish, oysters, and sea cucumbers. Commercial fishing has deteriorated dramatically in the last few decades. Only a few hundred fishermen still engage in this activity. They are concentrated near the port city of Massawa. Going out in small, often unseaworthy boats and using rudimentary equipment, they catch enough to feed their families plus a little more to sell in the market.

Recognizing the potential of the rich marine life along the country's coastline, the government set up the Ministry for Marine Resources to maximize revenue from offshore fishing and fish processing, while protecting and preserving marine resources through nature reserves. A US$4-million project was initiated in conjunction with the United Nations to provide new facilities for building boats and training fishermen and to make suitable arrangements for storing and distributing fish. Boosting the fishing industry will enable fishermen to support themselves and lessen malnutrition among the coastal communities, who have not recovered from the war.

INDUSTRY

Many of the big names in the Eritrean economy originated in the Italian colonial era, which saw a considerable rate of industrial expansion. Many of these factories were concentrated in Asmara, and they churned out food products, beer, tobacco, textiles, and leather goods. Eritrea soon acquired a reputation for producing shoes of good quality. The native workforce at that time learned skills that helped them find jobs abroad when they left their country during the war years.

Manufacturing today accounts for 20% of the country's GDP. Light industrial output consists primarily of foods, salt, textiles, and leather goods produced by both public and private small- to medium-scale enterprises located mainly in Asmara. Most of these factories are merely producing domestic substitutes for foreign products but are working to become more productive by modernizing facilities and training labor.

Heavy industry consists of salt and cement plants near Massawa and a petroleum refinery in Assab, which was built by the former Soviet Union when Ethiopia controlled Eritrea. The rebuilding of the Massawa-Asmara railroad will be one of the most demanding infrastructure projects in the country to date. Originally built by the Italians, the railroad was totally destroyed during the war for independence by Ethiopian soldiers, who used the rails to build trenches. The government has decided to employ the expertise of the original railway builders in the restoration project. When completed, the railroad will give a big boost to the economy.

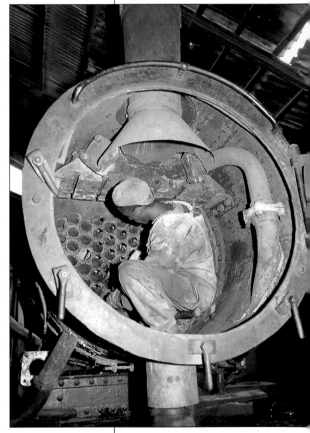

Above: **A laborer working in a railroad workshop in Asmara.**

Opposite: **A fisherman casts his net into the sea.**

MINERALS

Eritrea has substantial deposits of many minerals. Salt is found in abundance. Vast salt flats lie like ice-covered lakes in the area around Assab, in Massawa, and in the Kobar Sink in the Denakil Depression. Salt mining is a traditional occupation for Eritreans living in the Southern Red Sea region. Miners dislodge slabs of solid salt during the dry season and sell the crude blocks at the markets in Assab and Massawa.

Other commercially viable minerals found in the country are the metallic ores of gold, silver, copper, zinc, lead, and iron, and industrial minerals, such as sulfur, feldspar, gypsum, silica, and potash. Of these, gold shows the best prospects. The government has thus licensed the Ashanti Goldfields of Ghana to explore for more of this precious metal. In addition, deposits of granite, marble, slate, and limestone can be quarried for use in the construction industry.

The proximity of the oil-rich Arabian Peninsula has raised hopes of finding petroleum in Eritrean territory. Although efforts since the days of Italian rule have been unproductive, surveys have indicated the presence of oil and gas deposits in the Red Sea. The government has signed a deal with Anadarco Petroleum to explore the area.

TRADE

Eritrea has an unfavorable balance of trade, importing much more than it can export. Moreover, it exports mostly low-value goods, while importing expensive products. In 1996 the country exported an estimated US$95 million worth of livestock, sorghum, textiles, foods, and small consumer products. The same year, Eritrea imported processed goods, machinery, and petroleum products to a total worth of about US$514 million, more than five times the overall value of exports.

Eritrea's largest foreign market is Ethiopia, which absorbs about two-thirds of its exports. This is largely due to Eritrea's acceptance of Ethiopian trade through the port of Assab, which is Ethiopia's only avenue to the Red Sea. Other destinations for Eritrean goods are Sudan, the United States, Italy, Saudi Arabia, and Yemen. Eritrea imports from Ethiopia, Saudi Arabia, Italy, and the United Arab Emirates.

Independent Eritrea was born free of external debt. Within three years, however, a debt of US$46 million was amassed.

Opposite: **A hot spring spurts sulfur in Dallol in the Denakil Depression.**

ERITREAN MONEY

The Eritrean currency is the nakfa (Nkfa). One nakfa equals 100 cents. Notes come in denominations of 1, 5, 20, 50, and 100 nakfa, and coins come in denominations of 1, 5, 10, 25, 50, and 100 cents. One side of the notes depicts children and young women, while the reverse side has scenes from various parts of the country. The introduction of the nakfa as the Eritrean currency in 1997 was a double disappointment for Ethiopia. Besides replacing the Ethiopian birr formerly used in Eritrea, the new currency went by the name of the town where the Ethiopian army had sustained the most casualties. For Eritreans, however, the town of Nakfa represents freedom and happiness.

Passengers pack an old bus in Keren.

The 45-mile (72-km) Asmara-Massawa cableway took two years to build and required 3,900 metric tons of cables and other materials. Powered by eight stations and traveling at 5.6 mph (9 kph), its 1,620 trolleys transport 720 tons of cargo every day.

TRANSPORTATION AND COMMUNICATION

A strategic location on the Red Sea endows Eritrea with a natural potential to be a communications hub for northeast Africa. The ports of Massawa and Assab serve as gateways to many of the neighboring lands. Direct access to an international shipping route extends Eritrea's reach to regional and global markets. Ethiopia, for example, with its guaranteed use of the port of Assab, is a major regional market for Eritrean exports. Global transportation and communication is also possible from Asmara. An airport and telephone service equip the Eritrean capital with international connections. Another international airport is being constructed 8.2 miles (13 km) northwest of Massawa.

Improving internal transportation and communication networks is a priority for the government. Telephones are available in the major towns, but national penetration is low at about four telephones to every 100 families. The government is seeking international offers to improve the system.

One way to move around the country is on the Massawa-Asmara train. The railroad is, however, still undergoing reconstruction. Paved roads linking the major towns are in a generally bad condition. Intercity buses have no fixed timetable and depart only when they are filled. Long journeys break once or twice along the way for refreshments and visits to the restroom. Children ride free and share a seat with their adult companion.

There are buses in the major towns, but Eritreans tend to walk a lot. Asmara also has a fleet of decades-old taxis catering to the commuting needs of residents. Rural transportation features camels and donkeys.

ECONOMIC OPPORTUNITIES

The Eritrean government does not believe in accepting handouts from rich countries or nongovernmental organizations. It prefers to attract long-term foreign investment to build domestic infrastructure and thus facilitate economic recovery. Having identified tourism as a potential growth area, the government has opened much of the tourist sector to operation by foreigners. For example, American investors are helping to develop resorts on the Dahlak Islands.

American funds and knowledge first entered Eritrea with the establishment of a Coca-Cola plant. Italian expertise has also been sought in getting the manufacturing sector back on its feet. The World Bank is helping the country set up a vehicle assembly plant. The Investment Center mediates between foreign investors and the relevant government ministries. The inflow of funds increased until 1998, when the border conflict with Ethiopia put a dent in investor confidence in Eritrea.

A hotel in Massawa. The government has sold several hotels in Asmara and Massawa to foreign enterprises.

ERITREANS

ERITREA HAS A SMALL POPULATION of about 4 million people. A vast displacement of Eritreans occurred in the 1960s and 1970s, with many families taking refuge in neighboring Sudan and Saudi Arabia as well as far away in North America and Europe. Most Eritreans who sought refuge in the West have set up permanent homes there. They now constitute Eritrea's diaspora. While many Eritreans who fled to Sudan have returned, a significant number still await repatriation.

Eritreans are a diverse people, with many languages, cultures, and religions. Nine main ethnic groups inhabit different parts of the country, but they live in relative unity, having fought a common enemy together for the common goal of freedom. Ethnic friction is thus almost nonexistent, and the constitution allows no discrimination against any group. Today, Eritreans show solidarity in their desire to develop their country.

The population grew by 4% in 1999, an improvement over the war period. However, there are still many infant deaths, and the average life span is only about 56 years.

Left: **Children of Afar ethnicity in front of their hut.**

Opposite: **A woman from the Rashaida tribe in traditional head dress.**

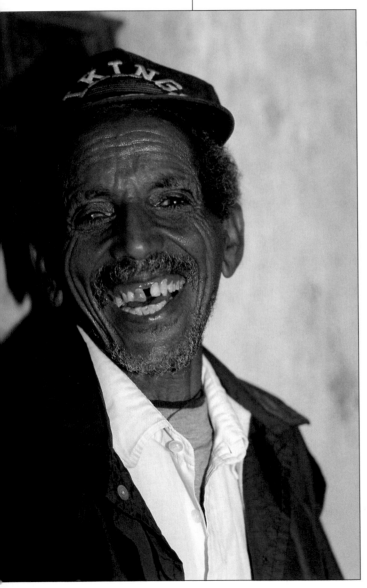

TIGRAY

The nearly 2 million Tigray in Eritrea constitute about half the country's total population. Living in the southern highlands, they speak Tigrinya and are mostly Christian. Descendants of early Semitic settlers in the Horn of Africa, the Tigray are related to the Sabean people referred to in the Koran as "People of the Book," along with Christians and Jews. One of their historical achievements was the setting up of the ancient empire of Axum. The Eritrean Tigray share this ancient heritage with the over 4 million inhabitants of the Ethiopian region of Tigray.

The Tigray are a beautiful and hardworking people whose determination contributed significantly to their country's attainment of freedom. Today, they are helping to build Eritrea with the same perseverance. Their spirit of sacrifice is also noteworthy, and they are likely to go hungry and offer their food to others who need it more.

The Tigray people are mostly peasants cultivating vegetables and grain in the temperate highlands. Coffee drinking constitutes an important part of their social life, and the women have a strong penchant for jewelry. The Tigray also have a rich heritage in music, featuring drums and string instruments.

TIGRE

Numbering almost 700,000, the Tigre constitute the second largest ethnic group in Eritrea. Although they go by a similar-sounding name, the Tigre people are different from the Tigray: the Tigre are descendants of the ancient Egyptians, profess the Muslim faith, and lead nomadic lifestyles.

Scattered in the northern highlands and on the eastern and western lowlands, many Tigre people have gradually moved to Sudan in search of water and pastures. Traditionally a nomadic tribe, they roam the countryside with their herds of goats, sheep, cattle, and camels, which they sell in the markets when they need to buy other essential items. A small number of the Tigre are farmers. Living in round huts with cone-shaped roofs, they cultivate corn, sorghum, wheat, barley, and legumes for food. Many Tigre people depend on government aid to support their large families.

A Tigre family may offer a daughter in marriage to a man from another Tigre family to resolve a feud between the two families which would otherwise end in bloodshed.

Left: **A Tigre woman with her child.**

Opposite: **A Tigray man in Western garb.**

51

AFAR

Around 300,000 Eritreans of the Afar tribe live in the southern desert plains of the country. They are also known as the Denakil, after the region in which they live, but this term offends them. They claim their ancestry in Noah and are a proud and strong people known for being ferocious warriors. In his book *The Danakil Diary*, Wilfred Thesiger said that "no Danakil man may wear a colored loincloth, a comb or feather in his hair, nor decorate his knife with brass or silver until he has killed at least one."

Nearly all the Afar are Muslim. They are divided into two subgroups. The "red ones" (as translated from their language) are the powerful nobles living along the coast, while the "white ones" are the commoners living in the mountains and in the Denakil Desert.

The Afar build oval-shaped huts from palm mats and set up camps surrounded by thorn barricades to protect them from wild animals and enemy tribes. Most of the Afar are nomads who herd sheep, goats, cattle, and camels. The size of their herds indicates their wealth. Some of the Afar near the Red Sea coast make their living as fishermen as well.

The Afar have traditionally traveled beyond Eritrea into Ethiopian and Djibouti territory, where another 750,000 Afar live. However, disputes between Eritrea and neighboring countries over national borders have had a negative effect on the Afar's nomadic way of life. Much of the disputed land includes their traditional routes of travel.

BEJA

An ancient people scattered across the desert regions of Eritrea, Egypt, and Sudan, the Beja consider themselves descendants of Noah's grandson, Cush. Numbering around one million altogether, the Beja are the largest non-Arabic ethnic group between the Nile River and the Red Sea, and have settled in the region for over 4,000 years. More than 100,000 Beja inhabit approximately 20,000 square miles (51,800 square km) in the western plain in Eritrea. Thousands of Eritrean Beja were driven into Sudan during the war.

The Beja were a powerful people in ancient times. Having established their kingdom in all of Eritrea after the fall of the Axumite empire, they are in a sense the common ancestor of all Eritreans living today, although many of the later generations do not trace their roots to the original Beja.

There are two Beja tribes in Eritrea: the Ababda and the Beni Amer. These tribes are made up of clans varying in size from one to 12 families. The Ababda live in the far north of the country and manifest a strong Arab influence. The Beni Amer have developed a social system which resembles a caste system and which the government strongly discourages.

With small, strong, and wiry frames, long noses, and oval faces, today's Beja people are nomadic shepherds who live in portable tents built by the women. They are Muslims and speak the Beja language. Many are also fluent in Arabic or Tigre. The aim of most young Beja couples is to produce many male children and acquire many female camels.

The Beja like to wear their hair in enormous knots, earning themselves the nickname "fuzzy wuzzies."

Opposite: **An Afar man wearing a turban.**

The Rashaida are people of Arab origin.

ETHNIC MINORITIES

The Nara, Kunama, Bilen, Saho, and Rashaida make up about 15% of the Eritrean population and are mostly Muslims. They live in most parts of the country, except in the central highlands. The Nara and Kunama live in the western lowlands. Their strong physiques, which they have inherited from their Negroid ancestors, set them apart from the rest of the population. The Bilen are mostly pastoralists who live in the northern highlands, mainly around Keren. The Saho reside on the coastal plain south of Massawa, quite close to the Afar. The Rashaida roam the northern hills and are the only true nomads in Eritrea. A small group of Nigerians live near Teseney. Their ancestors settled there on the way to or from the Muslim holy city of Mecca in Saudi Arabia. Ethiopians, mostly of Tigray heritage, form a small and dwindling minority in Eritrea's ethnic mosaic.

WOMEN

Of the 60,000 fighters killed during the war with Ethiopia, one third were women. Women made up 40% of the 95,000-strong EPLF army. Many of them fought at the front line during the liberation war, while those who stayed in the villages took over the jobs and roles of the men who had left to fight.

Returning from the war, however, Eritrean women saw their status decline. Some female fighters were considered unmarriageable when they returned to their native villages. Their independence and modern ways clashed with the traditional rural lifestyle. Many village families consider their daughters farm and home laborers, and keep them out of school. Polygamy and arranged marriages also continue to restrict women in Eritrea.

Eritrean perceptions of women are slowly changing with the example of female pioneers. Tirhas Iyassu, one of the best female painters in the country, paints images of men looking after children or cooking, to promote gender equality. Woizero Askalu Menkerios, president of the National Union of Eritrean Women, led a delegation to the fourth World Conference on Women in Beijing, which adopted an action program to improve the welfare of women around the world.

The Eritrean government recognizes the role of women in national development. President Afwerki has appointed three female ministers in his cabinet, and there are women holding other senior government positions as well. The government also actively supported the first Girls' Conference in the country in 1997 to encourage young girls to break out of their society's patriarchal mindset.

A veteran fighter from the liberation war lives with the consequences of her contribution to the country's 30-year struggle.

Women made up 48% of the commission that drafted Eritrea's first constitution.

55

THE REFUGEE PROBLEM

Around 750,000 Eritreans had to leave the country during the liberation war. Half a million went to neighboring Sudan, 75,000 to the Middle East, and 25,000 to Europe and the United States. Most had to battle inhuman conditions in order to reach safety. Traveling at night on camel-back or even on foot, many families fled to Sudan or

Djibouti. Parents sent their children away to protect them from abuse by the Ethiopians or from conscription into the guerilla army.

The refugees in Sudan lived in overcrowded camps with very few amenities. Life there was harsh, but far better than the life they had left behind in Eritrea. In the camps in Sudan each family had a hut with a little land to cultivate. The refugees organized their own communities, running schools for their children and rearing animals and crops for food. They earned a salary if they held a job in or outside the camps. The women formed self-help groups to make handicrafts, which they sold for money. The more educated refugees even managed to find sponsors, usually from Christian organizations, to finance their migration to the West.

When the EPLF liberated most of the country in 1989, Eritrean refugees immediately began to return home by the thousands. The Commission for Eritrean Refugee Affairs managed the repatriation process and reintegrated the returnees into Eritrean society. Between 1989 and 1992 more than 80,000 refugees returned to Eritrea, with 80% coming from Sudan. This sudden influx was a strain on the new country. Housing and social services were overstretched. There were not enough work opportunities for all the returnees, many of whom did not have the necessary skills to help the country develop economically. The government has started a scheme that tries to educate former refugees to help them get a job or start a business. Those with good business plans can apply for low-interest loans from the government to finance their start-up. While ex-fighters make up the new political class, returnees have taken over the economy of the country, going into business and setting up new enterprises.

Nearly ten years after liberation, the refugee problem has not been completely resolved. An estimated 100,000 Eritreans are still awaiting repatriation from camps in Sudan. Because of friction between the two governments, and despite efforts by the United Nations High Commission for Refugees, Eritrean refugees in Sudan are in limbo, not knowing when they will see their homeland again.

THE DIASPORA

The diaspora is a very important concept to Eritreans. It refers, in the collective, to all Eritreans who live outside their home country. Most of them escaped during the 30-year war with Ethiopia. Nearly a quarter of a million Eritreans reside in far-away countries, such as Australia, Canada, the United States, and Scandinavia. Virtually every family in Eritrea has at least one member outside the country. Although members of the diaspora may have decided to settle permanently in their host countries, they still consider themselves Eritrean and raise their children with an Eritrean cultural awareness.

After liberation, many among the diaspora returned to Eritrea to help in its recovery, while others decided to stay in their host countries and help their home country in an indirect way. The latter regularly send money back to Eritrea, contributing substantially to the country's annual revenue. These worker remittances form a large and stable flow of income, without which the government would face even greater difficulty in implementing its massive infrastructural reconstruction program. Today, many Eritreans who left the country as young children come back as tourists, to visit aged relatives and commune with the country of their birth. Some parents also send their foreign-born children back to Eritrea, so that they can experience hardship and not take life for granted.

One group that would like to return, if they had the means to, are the Eritrean maids in Italy. Although they earn a humble salary, they still send money back to their country of origin and help raise funds through activities such as the Bologna Festival.

Eritreans forced to leave Ethiopia return home to a joyous welcome. The border conflict between the two nations has led to over 720 Eritreans being expelled from Ethiopia.

LIFESTYLE

THE MAJORITY OF ERITREANS lead lifestyles that have changed little since Biblical times. Many tribes still live as nomads, almost untouched by Western civilization, and follow ancient customs and traditions. A wide divide exists in the way people live, especially between the urban and rural areas of Eritrea. Yet, even the cities look as if they had just emerged from a time warp, after 30 years of war.

In the last few years there have been massive reconstruction projects in the urban areas, in a bid to catch up with the rest of the world economically. In the rural areas people struggle to eke out a living from meager resources. Many survive only with government aid. The government aims to equip every child in the country with a basic education and to improve living conditions in most areas by installing basic facilities, such as piped water and electricity.

An Emergency and Recovery Action Program costing close to $2.5 billion was introduced after independence to develop the country's devastated transport, agriculture, and industry sectors.

Left: **Builders surveying construction plans in Asmara.**

Opposite: **An Afar woman grinding corn.**

59

Out of every 1,000 babies born in the country, an estimated 77 die within their first year of life.

THE ERITREAN FAMILY

An Eritrean woman bears, on average, six children in her lifetime. But not all of her offspring survive to adulthood. The high birth rate balances the high infant mortality rate and short life expectancy. Nevertheless, the Eritrean family remains relatively large by Western standards.

The father is the head of the household and the main breadwinner. If he loses the capacity to perform this role, his family is considered cursed. The mother feeds the family and does the household chores, usually with her daughters' help. Women and girls do all the laborious jobs, like tending the vegetable garden. They sometimes walk more than two hours each day to bring water home from the well.

Right: **An Eritrean farming family.**

Opposite: **A Rashaida man with his daughter.**

Both father and mother rarely play with their sons and daughters. However, they do tell their children traditional stories and teach them the names of their ancestors to pass on their cultural heritage. The mother showers her children with love and care, while the father is the disciplinarian and spends little time with his children. Eritrean men do not relish having daughters, girls being less valued than boys in their society. However, the father-daughter relationship is safe from the tension that tends to build up between the father and a son who tries to assert himself.

Many children in Eritrea have lost both their parents to the liberation war. Most of them now live with their relatives, supported by a little financial aid from the government. In urban centers most young people are marrying late, taking time to enjoy their new-found freedom and occupying themselves with hobbies and sports. In traditional communities, however, girls barely out of childhood are married off, sometimes to men old enough to be their fathers. Some Muslim ethnic groups also practice polygamy.

Every Eritrean has a first name, by which he or she is known, followed by the father's name, which women keep even after marriage.

A Tigre hut is round with a cone-shaped roof made from palm mats.

LIFE IN THE VILLAGE

About 80% of Eritreans live in the countryside. They generally build round huts out of stones, clay, and palm leaves. These can last up to 10 years if the palm is of good quality. On average, it takes four men to build a hut in one day. The shape of the hut and the materials used vary slightly according to the location, lifestyle, and heritage of the tribe. A Nara village, for example, looks like a colony of beehives, as the roofs of the huts reach to the ground. Each Nara family has three huts: one for the males, one for the females, and one used as a kitchen.

Rural life is slow and peaceful, keeping with the pace of nature in the raising of crops and livestock, but it is not an easy life. The people work hard to grow enough grain and vegetables and raise enough sheep and cattle to feed themselves, and the periodic droughts and famines bring great suffering. Still, there are occasions to celebrate, such as weddings and major festivals, when the whole village comes together in ritualistic ceremonies.

TRADITIONAL WEAR

Women clothe themselves in long, flowing, colorful dresses. A light shawl covers their head and drapes around their shoulders. Many Tigray women wear their traditional dress to festival celebrations and at their wedding. This long, white gown is embellished with golden embroidery around the cuffs and down the front.

Gold sandals are the traditional feminine footwear, while gold jewelry forms a major part of the complete attire. Eritrean women love jewelry. Their earrings, necklaces, rings, arm bands, and bracelets used to be made of silver or wood, but the preferred material now is gold. Decorative tattoos are very popular in the villages. Many women tattoo their gums using thorns dipped in charcoal dye to make their teeth appear whiter. The traditional hairstyle

is called *quno* ("KOO-noh"). Fine braids of hair stick close to the scalp and spray out from the nape like a giant fan.

Men in the countryside, especially in the hot regions, wear the *djellabia* ("JEL lah bay-ah"), a loose, long-sleeved robe made of white or light-colored cotton, over loose cotton trousers. They walk in leather sandals or rubber slippers. Muslim men complete the outfit with a turban. Men on the coast walk bare-chested, with a sarong, a large piece of cloth, wrapped around them from the waist down. The Beja and Rashaida nomads traditionally make their clothes from animal skins, but most of them now use commercially-manufactured fabrics. Eritrean boys mostly wear shorts and T-shirts, while girls wear little dresses, sometimes with a scarf. People in the cities, especially in Asmara, generally dress Western-style, that is, shirts or T-shirts and trousers for men and skirts and blouses for women. Few women wear pants. Jackets are very popular among male Asmarinos.

Friends share a few drinks in a bar in Assab.

LIFE IN THE CITY

Homes in urban Eritrea tend to be small. There is a living room (which may double up as the children's room), a bedroom, a kitchen, and a bathroom. Most houses have electricity and running water. They are usually sparsely furnished and kept clean and tidy. In recent years apartment blocks have sprung up in Asmara. With two or three bedrooms, these new living spaces are to Asmarinos the epitome of gracious living.

In many households both parents work while the children go to school. If the mother does not have a formal occupation, she keeps herself busy with church or other voluntary activities. The children are free to play outdoors after school, and they can do so safely, even at night, thanks to a low crime rate.

Friends and neighbors often meet in bars and cafés to chat and have coffee. A favorite pastime is to stroll along the street in the early evening. Most people in the cities even prefer to walk to and from work rather than ride the buses and horse-drawn carts that run through the towns.

WORKING HOURS

According to a 1997 government regulation, all civil servants have to work about 45 hours a week. Office hours are Monday to Friday, 7 AM to noon, when there is a two-hour break for lunch, and then 2 to 6 PM. On Fridays the lunch break starts a half hour earlier, so that Muslim workers have time to go to the mosque for their weekly devotions. Some enterprises in the private sector still stick to the old system, working from 8 AM to 5 PM from Monday to Friday, and a half-day on Saturday.

There are no fixed working hours in the countryside, where the time it takes shepherds and farmers to perform their tasks depends on the season and on the condition of their animals and crops.

THE NOTION OF TIME IN ERITREA

"To an Abyssinian, an hour means the whole day." Italian ethnologist Alberto Pollera made this observation in the days before the colonists brought clocks to Eritrea. However, it is still the reality today in much of rural Eritrea, where tasks are carried out in nature's time. Farmers and shepherds have no need to rush in planting crops and grazing herds. Even in the cities people go about their tasks the traditional way, according to custom. For example, many of them prefer to meet in person than talk on the telephone. Nevertheless, the Eritrean people and government are generally quite punctual in their business and office conduct.

A teacher guides her Afar students at the Red Sea Mission School in the coastal town of Tio. Workers from developed nations bring experience and expertise to the growth of education in Eritrea.

EDUCATION

Only 20% of adult Eritreans are literate, and there are enough schools and teachers to cater to just half of the school-age population. Only 60% of primary school-age children and 53% of secondary school-age youths attend school in the country. Girls in the rural areas are less likely than boys to go to school.

Children in the lower grades study in their native languages. They gradually absorb Arabic and foreign languages, especially English, as they advance to higher levels. Children in the seventh grade and above take all their subjects in English, a legacy of the British protectorate years.

The government is taking measures to improve the country's education system. Teachers are attending summer courses to upgrade their skills, and more schools, including boarding schools, are being built. Qualifying grades for admission to the university have been set lower for girls than for boys, in order to attract more girls to higher education. The University of Asmara is strengthening its faculties through ties with US universities.

HEALTHCARE

Chronic drought and decades of war have taken a toll on the health of Eritreans. Land mines from the war tear off the limbs of wandering shepherds. Malnutrition stunts the growth of children. Malaria, bilharzia, meningitis, rabies, and tetanus affect both children and adults.

Only 7% of the rural population have access to safe water and fewer than 1% have adequate sanitation. Residents of the cities are far more fortunate, but they still face sad conditions. Only 60% have access to safe drinking water and 48% to sanitation facilities.

A network of clinics and small hospitals provide medical care around the country. Asmara has two main hospitals. While doctors make accurate diagnoses, they often lack the preferred medicines.

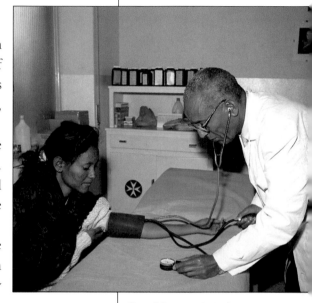

One of the more fortunate Eritreans who have access to modern healthcare facilities.

SOCIAL PROBLEMS

Fresh out of three violent decades, Eritreans have had enough unrest and are intent on rebuilding their country. As such, crime is not a serious problem. Petty theft does occur, but it is under control as most Eritreans are ready to help catch the thief. Neither is begging widespread, apart from children asking tourists for a few coins.

The main social problems are general poverty and poor living conditions, especially in the rural areas. The challenge to Eritrea is to unite efforts from the various ethnic groups to build the country's infrastructure and improve the lives of its people. With the government's stress on self-reliance and Eritreans' work ethic and nationalistic fervor, this is a challenge the country seems ready to take.

RELIGION

ERITREANS ARE ALMOST EQUALLY DIVIDED between Islam and Christianity. The Muslims are mainly pastoralists who live in the western plain and along the coast, while the Christians are largely Tigray peasants inhabiting the highlands. Islam entered Eritrea from Saudi Arabia across the Red Sea. The first converts were Eritreans living on the coast; the religion then spread through the lowlands. Christianity was introduced to the coastal areas in the fourth century and later spread to the plateau. Christians in Eritrea today belong to either the Ethiopian Orthodox Church or the Roman Catholic Church. There is also a small number of Protestants. Many of the smaller tribes retain their African animistic beliefs. The divisive potential of religion in the country has not materialized, partly due to the government's emphasis on equality among Eritreans. There is little, if any, religious animosity among the people.

Left: **The three main faiths in Eritrea coexist in Asmara. The towers of the Catholic Cathedral and the Khulafa el-Rashidin mosque stand behind the Inda Mariam Orthodox Church.**

Opposite: **A procession outside the Catholic Cathedral in Asmara.**

ISLAM

Eritrean Muslims belong to the less conservative Sunni branch of Islam. Those who live in the towns go to the mosque to worship every Friday. The small Khulafa el-Rashidin mosque in Asmara, built in 1937, overflows with devotees, who spill into the street and kneel on their prayer mats, oblivious to the city traffic. The lower part of the mosque's minaret is a fluted Roman column, which hints at the country's colonial past.

Religious observance is much more diluted in the rural areas. The mosques in Muslim villages do not look much different from the huts. Although most rural Muslims dress Arabic-style, the women do not cover themselves from head to toe.

Apart from the Afar, who are more religious, most Muslims in Eritrea do not know much about the Koran, the Islamic holy book, and do not follow Islamic religious precepts. They practice a folk version of the faith, following only some Islamic observances and retaining their pagan beliefs and customs. Most of them do not consume pork, but the same abstinence does not apply to liquor, which is also prohibited in Islam. Some ethnic groups practice polygamy, which Islam allows.

Islam

Muslims are well represented in all the towns in Eritrea, where they have made their mark in trade. The roots of their religion lie in some Dahlak Islanders, who converted to the faith in the eighth century. By the early 10th century, Massawa too had Muslim residents. However, it was not until the 16th century that Islam moved farther inland. Two factors contributed to this spread: the expansion of the Turkish Ottoman Empire into Eritrea and the forced conversions of thousands of Christians by Ahmed Gragn, the Sultan of Harar. Although Islam never displaced Christianity from the highlands, it continues to dominate the lowlands of Eritrea.

Below: **Muslims assembled in prayer.**

Opposite: **A mosque in Asmara.**

Above: **An Orthodox church.**

Opposite: **Women and men sit on different sides of the church.**

ORTHODOX CHRISTIANITY

Most Eritrean Orthodox Christians belong to the Ethiopian Orthodox Church. Eritrean Orthodox Christianity has its origins in the Syrian Orthodox religion of the fourth century. It displays some Jewish influences in the celebration of certain festivals, such as Meskel and Kidus Yohannes. Orthodox Christians in rural Eritrea also observe the Sabbath, the rest day for Jews from Friday night to Saturday night. However, the slaughtering of animals during religious holidays is a remnant of paganism.

The Ethiopian Orthodox Church is very well established in Eritrea, and church activities form a significant part of daily Christian life. A prominent icon in the Ethiopian Orthodox Church is the Ark of the Covenant, which contains God's Ten Commandments, according to the Bible. Although the Ethiopian Orthodox Church discourages reading the Bible, its followers accept the Bible as true, while also reading a few other books unique to their tradition. During festivals, such as Easter and Christmas, Eritrean Orthodox priests wear colorful and ornate robes and lead processions of devotees through the streets. Services are conducted in Ge'ez, the ancient language of the Axumite Kingdom. As the language is no longer used today, most priests are not conversant in it. Thus they often just memorize their parts of the service. Emotions run high during church services. Devotees embrace the walls of the church and kiss the ground.

Orthodox churches are usually built on a hill. The Debre Bizen monastery sits on a plateau at 8,041 feet (2,450m). It was founded by Abuna Filipos, who began his monastic life in 1361. The monastery survived Somali and Ethiopian invasions and holds 1,000 manuscripts in Ge'ez. The most important building for Eritrean Orthodox Christians is the Inda Mariam Church in Asmara. Built in 1917, it combines Italian and Ethiopian religious styles. Its twin towers are a useful landmark, and its interior is adorned with interesting murals.

The Ethiopian Orthodox Church has its own calendar. Each month has 30 days, and the extra days left at the end of the year make up a short 13th month. This calendar was used during the Ethiopian occupation of Eritrea. Since independence, however, the Eritrean government has replaced it with the Gregorian calendar used by most of the rest of the world.

The Catholic Cathedral on Liberation Avenue in Asmara. Its tall Gothic belltower is visible from anywhere in the city.

ROMAN CATHOLICISM

A latecomer in Eritrea, Roman Catholicism draws its followers from the Tigray and Kunama ethnic groups. The Roman Catholic Church has also attracted more converts in the towns, with its promise of higher education. The first Roman Catholic missionaries were Portuguese priests, who arrived in the 16th century. Their interest in Eritrea was political as much as religious. While trying to convert the population, they also helped the Abyssinians fight the invading Turks.

It was also through a missionary that Italy managed to get a foothold in Eritrea. One of the first Italians in the country was Fr Giuseppe Sapeto, who established a mission in Adua and helped the Italian government purchase land in Eritrea. With the setting up of the Italian colony in 1890, more Eritreans became Catholics.

Catholics in Eritrea are very devout and devote much time to church activities. Services are held weekly, on Saturday and Sunday, the same for the Ethiopian Orthodox Church. Conducted in Italian or Latin, services are joyful occasions, full of song and praise.

The Catholic Cathedral on Liberation Avenue in Asmara was built by Italian architect Scanavini in 1922. It provides a beautiful view of the city from the top. Atop the cupola is a statue of an angel cast in bronze.

In contrast with Muslim graves, which look like a pile of stones with some branches on them, Catholic graves are richly decorated with crosses and other sculptures. Catholic homes typically display a large amount of religious imagery, such as crucifixes and pictures of saints.

RELIGIOUS OBSERVANCES

The weekly worship day for Christians is Sunday. One day every month is also devoted to commemorating a saint or legendary king. The Copts believe that these monthly observances purge their sins, thereby easing their access to paradise. The most common of these holidays are: Micael, Gabriel, Medhanie Alem, and Be'ale Egziabiher. On these days believers go to an early morning service, then rest the day away, abstaining even from housework.

The saint's day is sometimes celebrated with a pilgrimage. The most colorful of these is the Mariam De'arit pilgrimage near Keren. On May 21 every year Christians flock to the town from all over the country to pray for miracles. A small shrine is set in a baobab tree some distance from the town. After the early morning service, cows and oxen are slaughtered, and a big feast takes place, lasting late into the afternoon.

Muslims also perform pilgrimages in honor of the descendants of Prophet Mohammed, although most of them are too poor to go to the holy city, Mecca. The most famous Muslim pilgrimage in Eritrea takes place in Keren. Believers first join in a feast of rice, cooked meat, coffee, and tea. Prayers are then said, after which the solemn atmosphere breaks into lively games and dancing. At the end of the day money is collected for the relatives of the prophet.

ANIMISM

Many Eritreans believe that evil spirits can take animal form to plague human beings with sickness and accidents. For example, the Tigre fear the evil spirit Zar, which they believe possesses people, sometimes driving them to their deaths. Only a shaman can enter into a trance and communicate with the spirits to exorcise demons and cure sickness. To protect themselves from spirits, believers in animism wear amulets, which sometimes contain verses of the Koran.

The various ethnic groups also have their own slants on animism. To the Afar, for example, trees and groves as well as the dead have special powers, and they hold an annual "feast of the dead" to appease the spirits of the dead. The Beja believe that some people have the power to curse others by giving them the "evil eye." The Nara and Kunama believe in a supernatural being in heaven called Ana, whom they pray to for blessings on their harvests.

Believers in animism also perceive droughts as a punishment for their sins. As such, they engage in rain-making rituals and slaughter livestock in the hope that their sacrifices will earn them forgiveness.

While animism is the indigenous belief system in Eritrea, some of its rituals, such as animal sacrifices, have also found their way into the local practice of "imported" faiths.

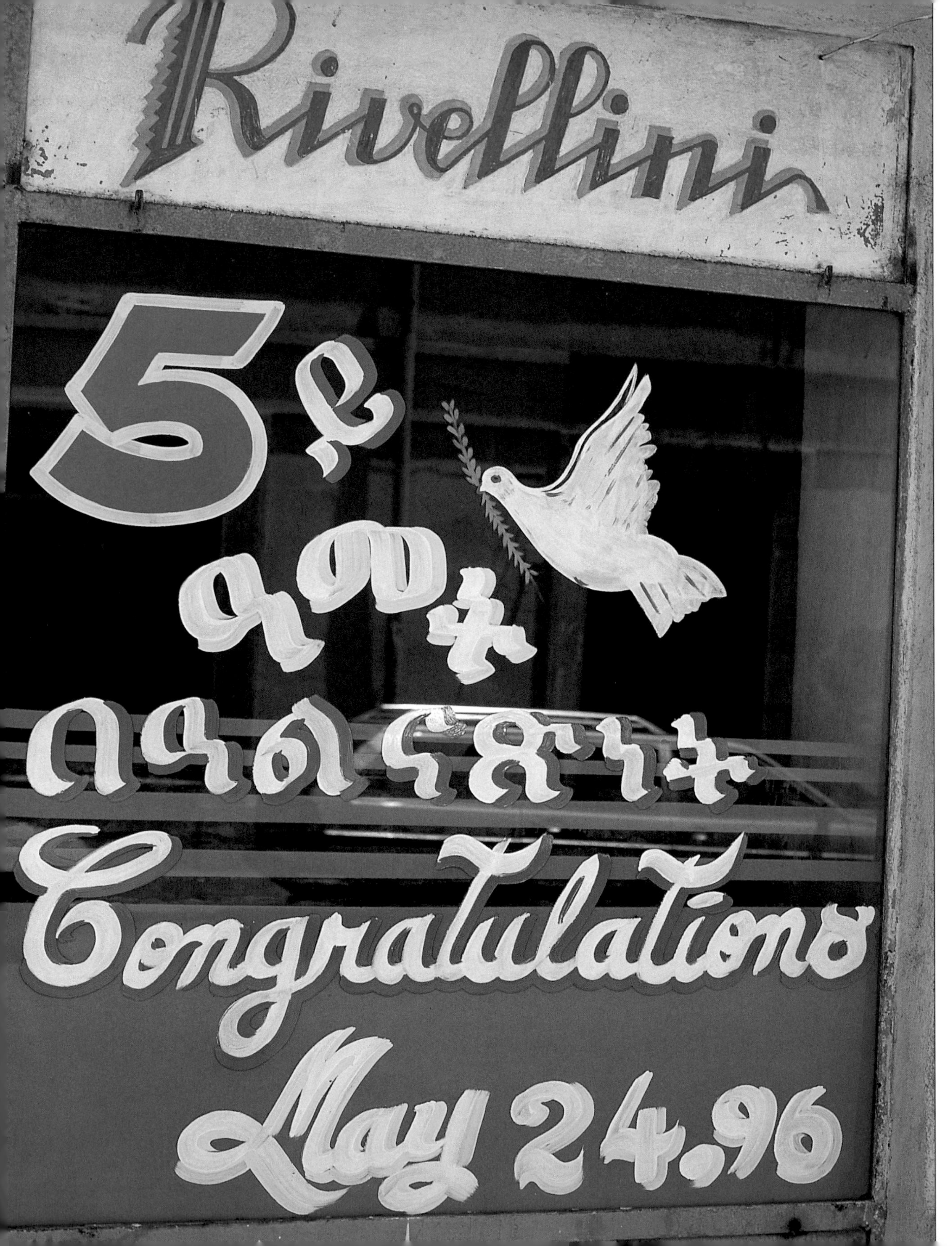
Rivellini
5ይ ዓመት
ብዓልናጽነት
Congratulations
May 24.96

LANGUAGE

ERITREANS SPEAK A NUMBER OF LANGUAGES depending on their ethnic and social backgrounds. Linguists have identified nine indigenous languages in Eritrea. There is no national language, but the working languages are Tigrinya, spoken by the Tigray ethnic group, and Arabic, spoken by the Muslim section of the population. The minority groups have their own languages and dialects, and many of their members speak Tigrinya or Arabic as well.

Eritreans are proud of their indigenous languages. During the years of the Ethiopian occupation, Amharic, the language of Ethiopia, was made the official language, and Eritrean languages were banned. But most Eritreans refused to speak Amharic. Instead, they continued to teach their native language to their children. Their attachment to Tigrinya became a political statement of their resistance to the occupation.

Left: **Eritreans having a friendly chat. The older generation, particularly in Asmara, still speak Italian inherited from their colonial past.**

Opposite: **A shop window in Asmara gives a mere glimpse of the linguistic diversity in Eritrea.**

A large signboard at the entrance of the port in Massawa reads "no smoking" in Tigrinya, English, and Arabic.

TIGRINYA

Tigrinya is a descendant of Ge'ez, an ancient language now used only in the Ethiopian Orthodox Church. Tigrinya is a guttural language that may sound quite gruff and harsh to those hearing it for the first time. Many Tigrinya words are pronounced at the back of the throat.

For the newcomer, Tigrinya is not just difficult to speak but difficult to learn as well. This is because it has many grammatical rules, and there is as yet no text that teaches the language phonetically. Tigrinya has its own script of over 200 characters, each representing a different sound. The consonants, like "g" and "k," are usually hard, and "r" is always slightly rolled on the tongue. The combination "ts" is sounded on the tip of the tongue as in the English word "pits." The vowels are pronounced either short or long. The letter "a," for example, is long as in the English word "hard" while the letter "e" is short as in the English word "bed."

Tigrinya was spoken and written possibly as early as the 13th century. However, the oldest available text is the *Code of Logo Sarda* from the 19th century. The language made considerable progress with the socio-linguistic work of European settlers in Eritrea and is now spoken by nearly half the population, specifically, the half that is of Tigray ethnicity.

A related language is Tigre, believed to be a direct descendant of Ge'ez. However, the two languages are not mutually intelligible. Tigre uses the same script as Tigrinya but varies in pronunciation and usage, depending on the geographical origin of the speaker.

ARABIC

Arabic is another Semitic language spoken by a significant proportion of Eritreans. It is the native language of the Rashaida tribe, and many Tigre speak Arabic in addition to their native tongue. The Muslim section of the population needs to know the language in order to read the Koran. Furthermore, the use of Arabic is spreading in the country, as refugees continue to return from Sudan and the Middle East, bringing with them their mastery of the language. Like Tigrinya, Arabic is full of guttural tones and sounds made in the back of the throat. The language contains three short and three long vowels. Words always start with a single consonant followed by a vowel. The Arabic script, consisting of 17 characters, is written from right to left. The addition of dots above and below the characters produces a total of 28 letters in the Arabic alphabet.

Ancient South Arabic script at an archeological site.

Friends freely help one another, expecting no thanks in return.

COMMON COURTESIES

Eritreans are a hospitable people. They often approach foreigners in the street to ask where they are from and how they like Eritrea.

The expected greeting at formal meetings is to shake hands with each person, asking about his or her health and family. In more casual circumstances Eritreans wish one another *selam* ("peace"). Close friends of the same gender kiss each other on both cheeks. Former fighters, however, have the most unique greeting style: they clasp their right hands together and bump their shoulders three times. In Arabic-speaking regions friends who have not seen each other for a while greet by touching right cheeks, then left cheeks, and right cheeks again.

Eritreans rarely thank others for little favors. This is perhaps because the literal translation of "thank you," *yekeniely* ("YUH-ke-nee-lih") in Tigrinya, sounds too solemn for everyday situations. Besides, Eritreans do not expect thanks for the small favors they do for others. Most of them take mutual help among friends and acquaintances for granted.

MINORITY LANGUAGES

Each ethnic group in Eritrea has its own language. Apart from Arabic, Tigrinya, and Tigre, all other languages in Eritrea are spoken, substituting the lack of their own script with Latin or Arabic script. These minority languages belong to two main groups, the Cushitic and Nilotic, but they may share no similarities, even within their language group. Furthermore, each language may have several dialect variations.

Afar, Beja, Bilen, and Saho are Cushitic languages. Afar and Saho are close relatives. Beja is considered one of the oldest languages in the Cushitic group. It is interesting to note that in the Beja language, the word "Tigre" means "slave." For the Beja people, the Tigre language itself is associated with being a servant. Bilen, spoken mainly in and around Keren, uses Ge'ez script.

Believed to be among the earliest languages in Eritrea, Kunama and Nara belong to the Nilotic group. Although both use Latin script, the two languages are mutually unintelligible, and Nara speakers speak Tigre or Arabic to communicate with the Kunama. There is considerable dialect variation within Nara. While some languages spoken in Sudan are related to Nara, Kunama has no known related language. There are some who consider Ilit, spoken in a region in the western lowlands, to be a relative, but others describe Ilit as a Kunama dialect. Barka is the main Kunama dialect and is understood by all Kunama Eritreans.

Most minority language speakers are bilingual, especially those who have attended high school. Bilen youth, for example, mix their speech with Arabic. In general, Bilen Christians speak Tigrinya in addition to their native language, while the Muslims speak Tigre or Arabic. Within their community, for example, 60% of the Christians are bilingual in Tigrinya, and 70% of the Muslims are bilingual in Tigre.

There is a total of 12 languages in Eritrea, one of which is no longer in use. This linguistic diversity spreads beyond the nine native tongues to include the foreign Italian and English, legacies of the country's colonial and protectorate years.

The use of English will grow as the urban world of business and technology gradually spreads through this developing nation.

FOREIGN INFLUENCES

The most lasting foreign influence on Eritrean languages is Italian. Many older Asmarinos use Italian in their everyday conversations with friends of the same age. Eritreans in general pepper their conversations with Italian words. Shop signs in Asmara and other big cities sport Italian names. However, it is in food-related industries that the use of Italian words is most pronounced, as Eritreans have adopted the Italian names for foods that do not feature in their traditional menu. This is done sometimes wholesale and sometimes with slight modifications. For example, "cheese" and "carrots" are *formaggio* and *carote*, exactly as in Italian, but tomatoes are *pommidere*, not *pomidoro*.

More and more English words are making their way into Eritrean speech today, especially in the fields of business and technology. The use of English will become more widespread in the country, as more children learn the language in school, and as the country progresses and opens up to the rest of the world.

MASS MEDIA

The Eritrean government exercises strict control over the media in the country. Dissension is not tolerated, and the media are expected to project the government in a good light.

The six private newspapers in the country print in Tigrinya. The government publishes one newspaper each in Tigrinya, Arabic, and English. *Eritrea Profile* is the only English-language newspaper. It contains news reports and cultural analyses, but also serves as a mouthpiece for the former EPLF and the PFDJ. Its electronic version is available on the Internet for the benefit of the diaspora.

The country has a government-owned television station and two A.M. radio stations. Television broadcasts reach only the urban centers for just a few hours a day. Eritreans living in the cities get to watch bulletins from international agencies like CNN and BBC, but only after they have been reviewed by the government. Radio reaches most of the rural population and is the best way to disseminate information and promote education.

Neighbors listening to a radio program.

Some stores in Asmara sell Time *and* Newsweek *magazines, while the top hotels sometimes make foreign newspapers available to tourists.*

ARTS

ERITREA IS AN ANCIENT LAND with many archeological treasures. Rock paintings, pottery, and calligraphy from the times of the country's early inhabitants provide the present generation with clues to their ancestry.

However, 30 years of fighting foreign oppression have distracted Eritreans from their rich ancient history; they are focusing their attention on building their economy, and progress in the arts has been minimal. The little artistic expression that surfaced during Ethiopian rule was limited to nationalistic images of fighters and patriotic songs of protest. Most of the artists in the country today draw inspiration from their struggle for freedom and still define themselves as witnesses of the liberation war.

Nevertheless, the collection of diverse cultures in this new nation has sustained the existence of a colorful tapestry of traditional handicrafts, music, dance, paintings, and poems. The various foreign influences since the time of the Turkish invasion have also left their artistic imprint on the architecture of the old buildings that still stand in the main towns. The colonial era, in particular, saw a blooming of the arts, with a distinct penchant for Italian styles.

As Eritrea develops economically and the population moves away from the mentality of oppression, local artists are finding more room and opportunity to express themselves, not only to their fellow citizens, but also to the world at large. The government is encouraging painters, writers, musicians, and actors to venture away from themes of war and explore a wider range of ideas and emotions.

Above: **An ancient three-necked pot on display in the National Museum of Eritrea.**

Opposite: **An old woman sews shells onto a traditional baby carrier.**

PAINTING

Most contemporary paintings from before 1983 portrayed the ubiquitous EPLF flag or the body of a dead soldier. They were a very effective medium of propaganda in uplifting the spirits of the people, but they did little to advance the cause of art. Eritrean artists did not start exploring their cultural heritage and local landscapes in their creations until Isaias Afwerki exhorted them to diversify their subject matter.

Most Eritrean artists have never received formal training beyond, perhaps, a few workshops under the tutelage of the EPLF army's single professional artist during the liberation years. Consequently, their straight-from-the-heart art combines raw, primitive talent with real, spontaneous emotion. During the war, painters coped with the scarcity of art materials by blending their own paints from leaves and using sacks of wheat flour covered in milk powder as canvases.

A painting portraying the people of Eritrea. Artists began to explore a wider range of subjects toward the end of the liberation war.

The Sawa National Service Camp contributes to artistic development among young men and women by providing them with supplies and lessons. Many budding artists only discover their talent when they touch paintbrush to easel, and some acquire enough artistic skill to eventually take on painting as a career. The EPLF art program has produced several professional painters, one of whom is Eduardo Araia, whose creations usually display a political sensitivity.

Habtom Mehret'ab is a prominent Eritrean cartoonist, who started drawing at age 11. He is also a painter, using people and landscapes as his subjects, and teaches art at the Asmara Model School. While his earlier cartoons contained political messages, his current ones portray the lighter side of life. They have appeared in several local publications.

Another store of paintings in Eritrea consists of the colorful murals that adorn the walls of the Ethiopian Orthodox churches and monasteries.

A mural in an Ethiopian Orthodox monastery.

LITERATURE

Eritrean literature is still in its infancy owing to the general absence of a literary heritage. Folk tales and legends have been passed down largely through oral tradition. Although the country has its store of scholarly writings, those from before the 20th century are in Ge'ez, a dead language that only Orthodox Christian Eritreans still come into contact with when attending church services. Books sold in stores are mainly in Tigrinya and Arabic, while books in English are available at the British Council Library and in stores in Asmara.

Prior to the country's liberation, the best Eritrean literary works were, ironically, written by foreigners. E. Litmann's *Publications of the Princeton Expedition to Abyssinia (1910–15)*, for example, is still the best collection of Tigre texts around.

The most prominent book in a local language is Kl'e Mensa, *written in 1913 by Karl Gustav Roden, a Swede.*

A girl concentrates on her work at school. Educating young people is important in developing a new, literate society.

ORAL LEGEND

Negusse Elfu is a legendary hero whose exploits are recounted in many poems among the Tigray people. The poems lament his death, and minstrels sing them in a sorrowful manner to the accompaniment of the local guitar and violin. Negusse was a rebel who left his native village to serve a foreign lord, rose in rank and power, and then returned to rule his native village. He died in his prime, by the hand of a traitor. Negusse's heroic deed was killing a lion. His destiny is captured in this folk ballad:

"O Negusse, Negusse son of Elfu,
Didn't you wield a two-edged sword, and fire a two-barreled gun?
Yes, you were mightier than the mighty
Oh Negusse, the pupil of my eye...

"O how large must have been their number, and how much evil their intentions
To have been able to overpower you, and to have slain you at last?
Now look what our people have done.
Yes, look what the fools have done.
When they could have tilled the land and traveled on it in quiet and calm
When they could have made themselves rich and gathered honey to brew their mead

"They chose instead to destroy their own fortress.
Whose fortress did they think they have destroyed
But their own mighty fortress and with it their pride.
Oh, Negusse see how vain is this world of mortals
See how they like to make fun, carrying your leather garment and sandals
To the village market along with your gun, where merchants bargain over your gown
Your blood-stained sword making news in town.
Alas, they think they could make a profit of sale
Nay, they only broke our own hearts, causing us to weep and wail."

Independent Eritrea is nurturing many native authors, who write in their native tongues. To cultivate local literature, the Eritrean Association for Development of Literature gives out annual awards to the best works by local authors. A big challenge for the country's writers is to break free from a national consciousness that still lies shrouded in the oppression years. High printing costs in the country are also a hindrance to publication for book authors, while poets and short-story writers may find their public forum only in magazines.

MUSIC, SONG, AND DANCE

The Asmara Music School had its first graduates in 1994. The school sprang from an EPLF project, initiated some 15 years earlier, which aimed to preserve the country's musical traditions by teaching children music.

Eritrean music uses a lot of percussion and string instruments. Drums are important in setting the rhythm for the melody provided by the *kirar* ("KEE-rahr") or the *chira wata* ("CHEE-ruh WAH-tuh"), the local guitar and violin respectively. The *kirar* has five strings and can play only five notes. Folk music is very popular in both the urban and rural areas. A performance is always well attended, and members of the audience often

A man beats a traditional drum to set the rhythm for ceremonial music.

90

show their enthusiasm and appreciation by climbing onto the stage to kiss and hug the performers. It is also common for Eritrean fans to dance and sing along with their music idols, or to stick banknotes on the foreheads or in the hands of the performers.

The first Eritrean to record Tigrinya songs on a compact disc is Abraham Afwerki. Now living in Italy, he is one of the most popular singers in Eritrea. Among his contributions to Eritrean music is his modification of the *kirar* to play 12 notes. The Abubaker and Stanley Band based in the Netherlands aims to gain international recognition for Eritrean pop music.

Eritrean dancing is mainly feet-shuffling and shoulder-jerking. It looks like a cross between African and Asian dance, accompanied by mild music with loud drumming. Every ethnic group has its own dance style, and the most beautiful dancers come from the Kunama tribe. They dance in couples, freely expressing their emotions through graceful, and sometimes suggestive, moves. Tigre and Bilen women dance the *sheleel* ("SHO-leel") in groups, swinging their long plaited hair vigorously across their faces.

A couple dances to clapping from the crowd.

The most revered singers in Eritrea are those who pioneered the resistance song against Ethiopian domination.

Colorful indigenous handicrafts are attractive items at the markets.

HANDICRAFTS

Every ethnic group in Eritrea has a handicraft specialty. The Nara tribe are famous for their saddles and baskets. Young Nara girls learn how to make coiled baskets from their mothers. These baskets are customarily made from natural materials, but contemporary versions have incorporated yarn in vibrant colors. The baskets are used at weddings and other celebrations.

Men in the Beni Amer ethnic group always carry on them a cross-shaped dagger, which they make themselves. A curved, two-edged blade and a big ebony hilt give the dagger a distinctive shape, which displays a strong Arabic influence.

Jewelry is another traditional handicraft. Silversmiths in the region around Keren create beautiful ornaments, which they sell in the market. Eritrean women of all ethnicities are very fond of silver and gold necklaces, bracelets, and belts.

This penchant for adornment that many ethnic groups in the country share extends to adding color wherever possible. Color is a defining characteristic of many indigenous handicrafts. Besides baskets, mats, and *injera* tray covers, even the clothes Eritreans wear display a myriad colors. Rashaida dress, in particular, is multicolored and decorated with beads. And baby carriers have shells sewn onto them.

Carvings are a traditional handicraft shared by all the ethnic groups in the country. Using basic tools and raw materials like wood and clay, sculptors create an assortment of figures including human and animal shapes, bowls, and trays. One of the best sculptors in Eritrea today is Kibrom Garza. He learned the art from the masters in his native village, and his works have attracted many admirers since he began as a young sculptor. His specialty is the *mido* ("MEE-doh"), a wooden comb traditionally worn by men in their hair. Kibrom does not sell his sculptures, and his *Massacre of Shiib* in soft wood is considered a masterpiece.

An intricate design in Arabic carved into the lintel on a building in Massawa.

Above: **A boy hugs a lute, one of many traditional musical instruments at the disposal of modern Eritrean theater.**

Opposite: **The children of independent Eritrea are a pool of promising potential for the growth of the new art form of theater.**

THEATER

During the war, the EPLF performed short skits all over Eritrea to stir up local resistance against Ethiopian oppression. However, the country has no tradition in drama. It is only today that theater is growing more popular in Eritrea as a channel of artistic expression.

Most plays presently running in the country are foreign classics performed in native languages. J.B. Priestly's *The Inspector Calls*, for example, played in Tigrinya in October 1997. Actors from the PFDJ Cultural Group displayed their talents on stage after two months of practice under a local director and with the support of the British Council.

Eritrea is, however, making progress in creating its own works for the stage. With a traditional foundation in dance and music, indigenous theatrical groups supported by international cultural organizations are gradually integrating native dance and music with modern dramatic skills. The various ethnic groups are also exploring their cultural heritage to write plays in their own languages.

The British Council is one of the most active foreign organizations that are contributing to the development of theater in Eritrea today. In 1997 it collaborated with two other foreign bodies to run two training courses for native artists. The first course trained Tigre and Bilen artists who then devised original plays which they performed for local audiences in various parts of the country. The second project took 12 graduates from a previous course to two villages to work with Tigrinya-speaking natives in developing homegrown theater. Leeds University has also sent representatives to Eritrea to carry out research on Tigre cultural performances.

Original Eritrean theater often takes the struggle against Ethiopian domination as a major theme. For example, the Eritrea Festival 2000 in Asmara showcased a musical theater performance called *Menfes Mekhete* (Spirit of Resistance). Focused on the fight against foreign oppression, the drama opened with a scene in which Ethiopian soldiers killed Eritrean civilians. There was no dialogue; instead the play used songs in the local languages, body gestures, colorful costumes, and lighting to convey its meaning. In one scene, actors dressed in red held lighted candles on their heads to represent those who had shed their blood in the liberation war and lighted the way for future generations.

Children's theater is budding under the guidance of Issayas Tseggai, a war veteran devoted to the cause of advancing Eritrean arts. Backed by the country's Ministry of Information and the PFDJ, he trained a group of Eritrean children for a theater festival in Ethiopia some years ago. The group has since blossomed into the Sewwit Children's Group, which Tseggai believes has now attained a standard high enough to perform on any stage in the world. He envisions them performing in Europe.

LEISURE

LIFE IS HARSH for the average Eritrean. Rural life presents few forms of leisure to choose from. Besides standard games like hide-and-seek, children may act out adult responsibilities, such as loading the camels or doing the household chores. Afar children play a form of chess using camel droppings. Town life features a wider range of recreational activities, such as relaxing at a café, watching a film, and shopping. Eritreans love the outdoors, too. Cycling and soccer are the country's top sports.

Special centers set up by the government promote sports and culture for young people. These occupy children and teenagers with healthy recreational programs, which equip them with useful skills and knowledge at the same time. Children would otherwise play in the streets, putting themselves as well as motorists in danger, and young Asmarinos typically roam the streets at night, attracted by the neon lights in the city center.

Left: **Afar children at play. Their favorite activity is rugby.**

Opposite: **Playing the harmonica is a form of leisure in the rural areas.**

RELAXING IN ASMARA

Asmarinos are far more fortunate than Eritreans elsewhere in the country. In addition to going to the movies and hanging out at cafés, they get to enjoy plays and exhibitions organized by the British Council. Concerts and dance performances by both homegrown and foreign groups also spice up the entertainment scene in the Eritrean capital.

The National Museum is a place of attraction for locals as well as tourists. It showcases artefacts from the excavations of the Axumite port, Adulis, scrolls in the ancient Ge'ez language, Italian paintings, and items from Emperor Haile Selassie's reign. The museum garden displays Italian cannons and machine guns.

Below: **The National Museum of Eritrea in Asmara.**

Opposite: **Inside the Asmara Theater.**

CINEMA

Going to the movies used to be considered a decadent activity, associated with a life of luxury. Since independence, however, the government has stressed the importance of film as a constructive art form with educational and recreational value. Ticket prices have been kept low to make movies affordable to more Eritreans. Movie theaters in Asmara, such as the one built in 1918 along Liberation Avenue, have been renovated to offer more comfortable seating and better projection equipment. The smaller towns, however, still make do with open-air cinemas. Owning a home video player does not seem to keep Eritreans away from the movie theaters, where they can catch the latest Hollywood blockbusters and Arabic dramas. However, tight censorship mercilessly cuts out scenes that are considered politically subversive or physically revealing.

The annual Asmara Film Festival was initiated in 1996 to encourage more Eritreans to go to the movies. Staged in collaboration with foreign embassies and various cultural organizations, the festival has screened films from the United States, Europe, Africa, and the Middle East, and has succeeded in pulling in the crowds to the movie theaters.

Young men learning metalwork under senior guidance.

YOUTH CLUBS

Government-run youth clubs are important meeting places for young people in the cities. They organize educational as well as recreational programs, such as woodwork or metalwork for young men and sewing or home economics for young women. Debates, quizzes, and other competitions test the members' general knowledge. The most popular activity, however, is soccer. The club in Massawa has 32 soccer teams consisting of players age 8 to 14.

Another very popular component of youth clubs is the video club. Members get to watch videos ranging from American adventure and romantic movies to educational documentaries on AIDS and birth control. CNN news broadcasts are recorded and shown in the evenings. The video clubs attract many viewers because few homes have a television set. Besides, the local television fare is quite limited. Club leaders advertise their video schedules in schools and around the city, often attracting up to 300 youths to their screenings.

COFFEE

A major social activity is the coffee ceremony. Making Eritrean coffee, called *bun* ("BOON"), is an elaborate affair. The preparation is always the woman's job. The hostess sets the mood by burning incense. Once everyone is seated, she sits down on a low stool and roasts the raw coffee beans in a shallow pan over a small charcoal fire. The smoking beans are passed around to the guests so that they can smell the aroma. Both the hostess and the guests use their hands to waft the smoke toward their faces.

When the house is filled with the wonderful smell of roasted coffee beans, the hostess grinds the beans in a mortar using a pestle. She then transfers the ground coffee into a round clay pot with a long neck and a tube-like spout. Some people add a little crushed ginger as well. The hostess pours water into the pot and brings the coffee slowly to a boil. Letting it boil over invites shame, so as soon as the mixture starts to boil, the hostess removes it from the fire, lets it cool slightly, and then returns the pot to the fire. She repeats this step several times to attain the desired strength.

After an hour, the coffee is finally served in tiny cups with lots of sugar. Popcorn is passed around to accompany the coffee. The entire coffee-making process is repeated as many times as it takes to ensure that all the guests have had their fill. Everyone should drink at least three cups and compliment the taste. A hostess may react to the lack of compliments from her guests by pouring away the prepared coffee and brewing a fresh pot.

Making coffee the Eritrean way.

CYCLING

Cycling is one of the most popular sports in the country. Cycling clubs are found everywhere, and many women also take the sport seriously.

The cycling federation organizes bike races at regional and interclub levels, as well as to celebrate national holidays. During these events, thousands of spectators turn out in the streets to cheer the racers on. One of the toughest races in the country takes place on the Asmara-Keren road. The 50-mile (80-km) route, which winds up and down steep slopes, tests and sharpens the skills of the best cyclists in the country. These go on to race in international competitions, such as the Tour de France or the Giro of Italy, which Eritreans watch intently at home.

SOCCER AND OTHER SPORTS

Soccer is another national obsession, although it is male-dominated. There are more than 200 soccer clubs and more than 5,000 registered players throughout the country. Eritreans do not play soccer professionally. Registered players hold regular full-time jobs and confine their training and matches to the weekends. The national federation organizes regional league and championship games for both adults and the youth, and matches are watched by thousands of ardent fans. Despite the lack of playing fields and sports equipment, almost every Eritrean male plays soccer with gusto. Soccer fanatics also follow the games of European clubs, especially the Italian ones, and international teams. The national soccer team takes part in the African championship and other regional tournaments.

Eritrea's track team has run races and marathons in the All Africa Games. The National Union of Eritrean Women has two volleyball teams, and the Asmara Volleyball Federation regularly organizes local tournaments. A basketball contest has even been organized for disabled war veterans living in Asmara.

Wealthy Asmarinos can play tennis at the club and go horseback riding. Eritreans have many good beaches in Assab and Massawa to go to for a swim in the sun. Many young people in the cities are also avid basketball players, being influenced by returnees from the United States.

A youth soccer event held recently at the Asmara Stadium brought together the capital's 147 teams, which consist of around 3,000 children between the ages of 8 and 15.

Left: **Ball games are popular among young Eritreans.**

Opposite: **Cycling, a common competitive sport, also has leisure and practical value.**

FESTIVALS

HOME TO A DIVERSE POPULATION, Eritrea celebrates many festivals during the year. Most of these are religious and traditional in nature. For example, the coming of the rains and the end of the harvest are causes for celebration among the farming population. There are also several secular national holidays, which mark significant events in the political and social history of the country, such as its independence day. An entire clan or village may also gather to celebrate milestones in the life of individual members.

The main ingredients for a complete festival are food, drink, music, and dance. Prayers and spiritual rituals form the focus of many celebrations, as religion plays an important role in Eritreans' daily life. Finally, feasting with relatives and friends top off the holiday. Christian festivals are generally full of pomp, while Muslim celebrations tend to be more muted.

While encouraging Eritreans to have fun, the government also advises them to reduce the wastefulness of feasting and drinking.

Left: **A tribal dance to celebrate the arrival of a new bishop in a village.**

Opposite: **The festival of Timket is celebrated by Orthodox Christians in Eritrea.**

CHRISTIAN HOLIDAYS

On festival day Orthodox Christians in Eritrea go to church in their best clothes. After the service, the priests lead the congregation in a street procession, and the rest of the day is spent feasting and having fun. The priests are always served the best food and wine at these feasts.

Timket, which falls on January 19, is the most important festival for Orthodox Christians in Eritrea. It commemorates the baptism of Jesus in the Jordan River. On Timket Eve people flock outdoors in lively and colorful processions. Then on the day itself the priests parade a small cloth-covered chest, symbolizing the Ark of the Covenant, through the streets. The congregation follows them to a pool or river to witness the reenactment of Jesus' baptism. They celebrate with a feast after the parade.

The festival of Meskel commemorates the finding of Jesus' cross by Empress Helena (the mother of Constantine the Great) about 1,600 years ago. On September 27 devotees plant a tree in the town square and later bring tall branches or poles with yellow daisies tied at the top to this location. After the church service, the priests lead the congregation to the bundle of branches in the square and set fire to it. Then everyone dances around the bonfire in celebration and song.

The Kunama call the holiday of the cross Mashkela. Kunama villagers carry lit torches in procession to a clearing outside the village. Here, they pile their torches in a huge bonfire and dance around it until the last ember flickers out. This is when they gather the new harvest and prepare a drink from the fresh grain to offer to their ancestors. Only after all these rituals have been performed do they eat of their harvest.

Catholic and Protestant Eritreans pay the most attention to Christmas. On December 25 they attend services at church and then go home to feast and exchange presents among family and friends. Those who can afford it put up a Christmas tree and perhaps a nativity scene.

Opposite: **Orthodox Christian priests wear colorful and richly decorated robes on festival days.**

HOLIDAYS IN ERITREA

The Eritrean government has declared 16 public holidays in a year. This number may seem large, but it is the only way to ensure that the various religious groups in the country are well-represented.

The national holidays are:
January 1: New Year's Day
March 8: International Women's Day
May 1: Labor Day
May 24: Liberation Day
June 20: Martyrs' Day
September 1: Launch of armed struggle

The fixed Christian holidays are:
January 7: Genna (Orthodox Christmas)
January 19: Timket (Orthodox Epiphany)
September 11: Engutatsh (Orthodox New Year)
September 27: Meskel (Finding of the true cross)
December 25: Christmas

The dates for Fasika (Orthodox Easter) and Good Friday (Orthodox) vary annually, as they follow the lunar, rather than solar, calendar. They are always celebrated in the spring. Muslim holidays also follow the lunar calendar. Id al-Fetr (the end of the fasting month) falls in the spring, while Id al-Haj (the pilgrimage to Mecca) and Mewlid al-Nabi (the birthday of Prophet Mohammed) fall in the summer.

ISLAMIC HOLIDAYS

During the feast of Sidi Bekri, pilgrims dance in a circle, taking turns to step inside where a man waits holding a cudgel. If a volunteer can endure the flogging without flinching, he takes over the cudgel, and a new round begins.

The three most important celebrations for Muslim Eritreans are Id al-Fetr, Id al-Haj, and Mewlid al-Nabi. Festivities for the first two can last up to 10 days in certain regions.

Id al-Fetr celebrates the end of Ramadan, the Muslim fasting month. For 30 days, all Muslims, except for the very young, the very old, and the infirm, eat or drink nothing from sunrise to sunset. This is a time given to prayer, meditation, and introspection. On the morning of Id al-Fetr, everyone puts on new clothes, children ask their elders for forgiveness, and the men go to the mosque for special prayers. When they come back, it is time to feast with relatives and friends. Some villages organize communal games and activities. The Beni Amer take part in camel races and competitions showcasing their swordsmanship and horsemanship.

Id al-Haj falls on the 10th day of the 10th month of the lunar year. It celebrates the pilgrimage to the holy city of Mecca, a pilgrimage that every Muslim endeavors to fulfil at least once during their lifetime. On this day Muslims believe that the gates of Heaven remain open for the faithful. Those who get blessings from their parents on this day are also blessed by God (or Allah). Animal sacrifices characterize this festival. Muslims slaughter sheep and offer the skins at the mosques. All families make it a point to visit their relatives on Id al-Haj.

Mewlid al-Nabi commemorates the birth of Prophet Mohammed. Although it is celebrated with as much fervor as Id al-Fetr and Id al-Haj, this is usually a solemn occasion. After morning prayers, all male believers gather together to enjoy cooked meat and dates with tea and coffee. The women stay at home to share a modest banquet. During Mewlid al-Nabi, Muslims recite a text entitled *Mewlid al Nabe*, which describes the birth of the prophet. They accompany their chanting with a dance.

NATIONAL HOLIDAYS

Eritreans devote three days each year to celebrate their nationhood. National Day falls on September 1, the day the armed struggle against the Ethiopian military regime was launched in 1961. Liberation Day, on May 24, commemorates the joyous occasion when the EPLF troops evicted the Ethiopian army from Asmara. Martyrs' Day, on June 20, remembers those who lost their lives in the fight for their country's freedom.

The program for these events contains speeches by the president and other leaders, public demonstrations, cultural shows, sports contests, seminars, and exhibitions. At the start of official celebrations, a group of religious leaders representing the major faiths says a prayer for the country and gives their blessings to the people. Public displays aim to reinforce Eritrean patriotism and to emphasize the need to be committed to rebuilding the country. As they celebrate their hard-won freedom, Eritreans are also reminded of the difficulties that lie ahead and of the contributions each of them has to make.

YOUTH FESTIVALS

Most festivals for children in Eritrea are religious in nature. Hiyo falls on the day after Christmas and commemorates the killing of infants by King Herod as related in the Bible. On Hiyo children visit villagers' homes and sing for a treat of roasted chickpeas. For Aba Abraham on

THE *DADDA*

The Nara of the Western Lowlands welcome the arrival of the rains in the winter with a five-day celebration. This celebration, called the *dadda*, is a form of prayer in the hope that the community will receive a bountiful harvest.

During the *dadda*, young men from two neighboring villages gather to perform a ritual fight. At the start of the rainy season, every young man makes two shields, one from the bark of a tree and the other from the hide of a giraffe. He also makes a stick from a special tree, and his girlfriend decorates his animal skin shield with beads. In the meantime, two elders from each village go up a hill, where they kill a goat, mix its blood with some medicinal herbs, and spray the mixture all around. The ground then becomes sacred, and no human or animal is allowed on it for the next five days.

After five days, the *dadda* begins. Accompanied by beating drums and dancing, the elders lead the young men up the hill. Dressed in only a short skirt, his hair smothered in ointment, each young man carries his shields up the hill. Before the fight, he gives the decorated shield to his girlfriend and takes up his stick and the other shield. At a signal from the elders, the young men begin the fight. They fight for an hour until the elders order them to stop. Then everybody goes back to their village, and the fighting resumes in the same manner the next day.

On the third day, the fighters meet near a big stream, where they shake hands and enjoy a big feast of barbecued goat prepared by the villagers. Then they go home, put on their best clothes, and dance the night away with the rest of the village. The next day, the warriors go into the forest and hunt rabbits. Then they bring the rabbits to the middle of the village and have yet another feast. On the last day, all the villagers gather with their cattle, bringing along some milk and loaves of bread. They pour the milk over the bread and plunge into the final feast of the festival before taking their cattle to the pastures. The *dadda* is now complete.

August 27 children parade through the streets with lighted torches. When they go home, their elders walk over the torches placed on the floor and pray for a bountiful harvest. Hoye, celebrated with burning torches, singing, and processions, takes place twice a year, on New Year's eve and Meskel's eve.

The festival of Aba Samuel spans two weeks in December. During this time, girls go singing from house to house and receive food and money in return. They use part of the money to buy food, which they offer to the church. The rest of the money they spend on food for themselves, and usually everyone else joins in the feast.

Children celebrate Youth Environment Day in a colorful assembly in Assab.

FAMILY CELEBRATIONS

Every milestone in the lifetime of the average Eritrean is celebrated according to Christian or Islamic traditions, and with singing, dancing, and merrymaking. Celebrations usually last several days.

For babies born into a Christian family, the first life event is baptism and name-giving. Baby boys are baptized at the age of 40 days, while baby girls are baptized only when they are 80 days old. Early in the morning, the mother dresses herself and her baby in their best clothes and goes to church together with the baby's godparents and some relatives. The baby is baptized and named following the church service, and then everyone shares some bread. At home the parents throw a lunch party, inviting friends, neighbors, and the priest who performed the baptism. The guests bring sugar and bread for the baby.

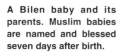

A Bilen baby and its parents. Muslim babies are named and blessed seven days after birth.

In Muslim households circumcision is the most important childhood event done usually at the age of 7. Girls are also circumcised despite the risk of severe injury if the operation is not done properly and in sanitary conditions. Circumcision of boys, however, is given more importance. Goats are slaughtered, relatives and friends come over with gifts, and much feasting takes place. In the evening the religious leaders arrive to do the operation, and the family offers them food, sweet syrup, and coffee. When girls are circumcised, only a few guests are invited, and only porridge is eaten. In some communities, the women even perform the ritual in secret.

Weddings usually take place in January, outside the harvest seasons and fasting periods. In the villages betrothals and arranged marriages are still the norm, and families sometimes look for their children's life partners within their own clan. The bride's family pays a dowry, and the groom's family pays a bride price of cattle, jewels, and dresses. While Christians marry in church, Muslims marry at home, with the sheik officiating. In Asmara wedding parties on hotel rooftops last late into the night.

Traditional wedding practices are waning as Eritreans gradually take to modern lifestyles.

FOOD

ERITREAN CUISINE IS AS VARIED as its people. Not only do the different ethnic groups living in the different parts of the country have unique food specialties, but they also prepare different versions of the same dishes.

However, Eritrea does not provide enough food to feed its entire population. Due to chronic drought, families living in the rural areas stare famine in the face each day of their lives, wondering when they will see their next meal and where it will come from. The majority of Eritreans depend on food aid from the international community, surviving on porridge made from ground grain, flour, and water. When they have nothing to eat, the poor fill their stomachs with anything barely edible, such as wild vegetables and prickly pears. People in the urban areas, in contrast, have access to a variety of foodstuffs. For example, the Asmarino diet features Western items like spaghetti and steak.

In Eritrea children and mothers with newborns are given the best nutrition. This includes meat and dairy products. Children in the cities also consume mashed potatoes, fruits, and honey.

Left: **The national dish—*injera* with spicy stews and sauces. Eritrean cuisine is as colorful as the people who create it.**

Opposite: **A chef at a restaurant in Assab slices meat.**

DAILY BREAD

A traditional Eritrean staple food is *injera*. This is a spongy, slightly sour pancake made from fermented teff, wheat, or sorghum. At mealtime, the family gathers around a large tray on which layers of *injera* lie topped with a variety of spicy stews and sauces. *Zigni* ("ZIHG-nee") is a chicken or beef stew; *alicha* ("ah-LEE-cher") is a vegetable stew; and *shiro* ("SHEE-roe") is a legume puree. Each person partakes of the meal by breaking off a chunk of *injera* from his or her side of the stack and using the chunk to scoop up some of the topping.

Another favorite staple is *kitcha* ("KIT-cher"), a thin, baked unleavened bread made from wheat or barley. In general, the highlanders consume teff, wheat, and barley, while the lowlanders cook with durra and millet. Also, more oil and butter is used in the urban areas, as those living in the rural areas cannot afford these items. Meat consumption is limited to the very wealthy in Eritrea. The poor get to taste meat stews only on festival days, when the village holds a feast. The most common meat is goat, but

116

the coastal populations also consume a fair amount of fish. Rural Eritreans get most of their protein from milk and legumes such as lentils. The poor living in the urban areas of the country substitute meat with beef tripe, which is cheap but difficult to prepare. Their alternative to *injera* is *shiro*. As this spicy porridge keeps for days, many working mothers cook a big pot over the weekend and then reheat portions of the *shiro* for daily meals.

Spices play an important role in Eritrean cuisine. In fact, all traditional recipes in the country require at least one type of spice, and most dishes are flavored with a combination of several. *Berbere* ("bear-BEAR"), a blend of numerous spices and dried chilies, goes into almost everything from *shiro* to *zigni*.

A spice seller at the market. Coriander, fennel, fenugreek, and red pepper are the most commonly found spices in Eritrean dishes.

SHIRO

(Serves six to eight people.)
1.5 cups oil
1 cup red onions, chopped
1 clove garlic, chopped
2 cups water
1.5 cups chickpea flour
A pinch each of cinnamon, fenugreek, coriander, fennel, red pepper
Salt to taste

Heat oil in a pan and fry onions and garlic until brown. Add water and bring to a boil. Sprinkle chickpea flour a little at a time, stirring constantly to prevent lumps. Add salt and spices. Cook until mixture is smooth and thick. Remove from heat. Serve hot or cold.

A man collects palm sap to make *douma*.

BEVERAGES

Eritreans consume water, milk, and a variety of traditional drinks. Muslims generally do not drink alcoholic beverages, sticking to coffee, tea, and other unfermented drinks. Highland Muslims have a preference for *aba'ke* ("ah-BAH-kay"), an unfermented drink made from a lentil-like grain. Linseed is also ground and mixed with water to make a refreshing drink.

Mead in Eritrea is a nonalcoholic honey drink. Its fermented version is *mies* ("MEES"). Because of the high cost of honey, it is not as popular as the other homebrew *suwa* ("SOO-wah"), a beer-like drink made from hops and a fine millet-like grain. *Zebib* ("ZAY-bib") is an anise-flavored liquor that Eritreans usually bring with them when visiting their friends or relatives. The Afar make a very strong alcohol, called *douma* ("DOE-mah"), from the sap of palm trees.

Fizzy drinks are also enjoyed by young and old in Asmara and other towns. Besides the ubiquitous Coca-Cola, Eritrean urbanites like to drink *spritzi* ("SPRIT-zee"), which is fizzy water flavored with fruit juice. Adults enjoy tea or espresso, always with a lot of sugar. In some areas coffee is served with ginger or black pepper as well as sugar. Blended banana, mango, or papaya juices are also common in the major cities.

TABLE MANNERS

Eritrean families eat communal-style, sharing food from a large tray placed in the middle of a low dining table. Among the Tigray especially, children and adults sit at separate tables, as the former are considered to have no table manners. Before a meal, one of the women of the household goes around carrying a basin of water, in which everyone washes their hands. This is because Eritreans eat with their fingers.

Then everyone sits around the table, either on the floor or on low stools, and the head of the family says grace. Each person takes from the portion of food closest to him or her, using only the right hand. It is bad manners to lick the fingers or to let them touch the lips, and it is rude to return leftover food to the communal tray. When dinner is over, the head of the family again says grace. Then the wife covers the tray with a conical lid and takes it away, amid murmurs of blessings and praises.

THE ERITREAN KITCHEN

Children enjoy a meal by themselves, away from the disapproving glare of adults.

Cooking is done by women only, especially in the rural areas. The kitchen is a small and dark space located in a small hut away from the living quarters. There is no running water, and one of the most important utensils is the water pot. Girls walk for hours everyday to fetch water from the communal well or tap. The stove is placed on the floor, and the cook either squats or sits on a low stool to prepare meals. Most rural kitchens are equipped with wood-burning stoves, while in the towns, people also use charcoal for fuel. Only the very rich families can afford gas or electricity.

Urban cooks use aluminum pots and pans, while many rural women still use utensils made of clay or wood. However, plastic spoons and bowls are fast invading rural kitchens. The mortar and pestle, a large ceramic or stone bowl and a long pole, have disappeared completely in the towns, but can still be seen in rural kitchens. Women spend a long time each day grinding the grains for making *injera* or porridge.

FRESH FROM THE MARKET

Fresh produce is obtainable from the many markets in both Eritrea's rural and urban areas. Large villages and small towns in the country hold weekly markets that attract people from places as far as 5 miles (8 km) away. These people come to sell their excess subsistence crops and home-reared livestock and to pick up food supplies. Eritrean markets have everything. While stalls selling meat, fruits, vegetables, grain, and spices are the focus of activity, market-goers can also find furniture, kitchen utensils, clothes, jewelry, and religious artifacts being sold at stalls standing on the outskirts of the main market. Surrounding the market in Keren, for example, are tailor shops and vendors of various handicrafts. Cattle and wood are traded at the edge of the town to avoid the animals causing congestion and inconveniencing the residents.

Asmarinos have the added option of patronizing supermarkets and grocery stores. The wealthier residents can even buy fine wines and chocolates from specialty Italian-style shops.

EATING OUT

Eritreans eat out mainly at lunchtime, when it is impractical to prepare their meals. Dinner, however, is usually eaten at home, as it is much cheaper to eat in. Only wealthy families can afford to dine out regularly. In the evenings the restaurants in Asmara and Massawa are mostly filled with tourists, foreign residents, and diplomats.

Most restaurants in Eritrea serve either local or Italian food. The fare may not always be of international standard, owing to the lack of trained cooks and high-quality ingredients. Far more popular than the restaurants in Asmara are the cafés that dot the city. Some of these open early in the morning to sell breakfast favorites, such as scrambled eggs with onions and tomatoes, called *frittata* ("FRI-ta-tah"), and *fool* ("FOOL"), a bean puree. Asmarinos love to sit at the sidewalk cafés, where they chat with their friends over coffee, watching the people and traffic go by. Many cafés are equipped with a television and video player, and this draws large evening crowds in for ice cream or after-dinner drinks.

Dining in restaurants is still a luxury few Eritreans can afford.

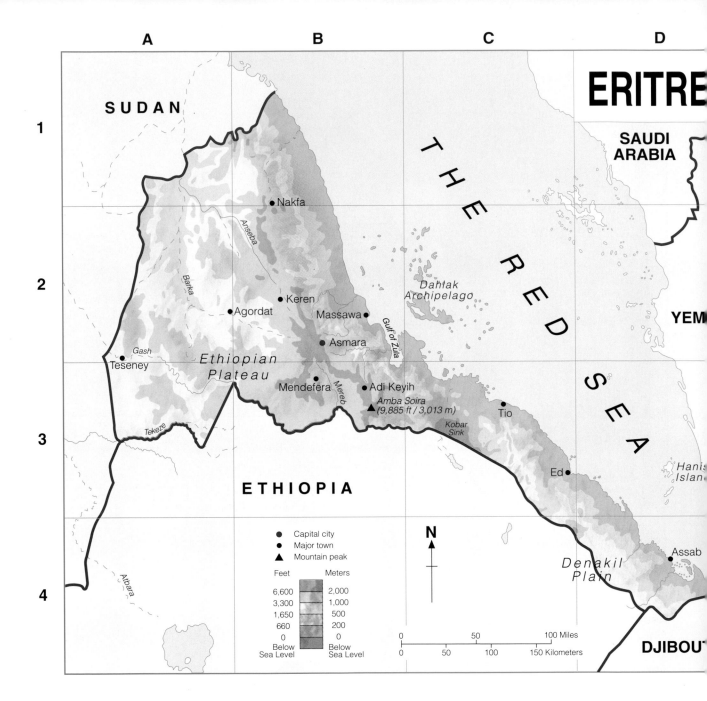

ERITRE

Adi Keyih, B3
Agordat, A2
Amba Soira, B3
Anseba River, B2
Asmara, B2
Assab, D4
Atbara River, A4

Barka River, A2

Dahlak Archipelago, C2
Denakil Plain, D4
Djibouti, D4

Ed, C3
Ethiopia, B3

Ethiopian Plateau, B3

Gash River, A2
Gulf of Zula, B2

Hanish Islands, D3

Keren, B2
Kobar Sink, C3

Massawa, B2
Mendefera, B3
Mereb River, B3

Nakfa, B1

Red Sea, C2

Saudi Arabia, D1
Sudan, A1

Tekeze River, A3

Teseney, A2
Tio, C3

Yemen, D2

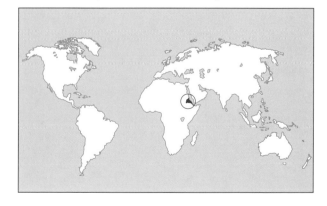

QUICK NOTES

OFFICIAL NAME
State of Eritrea (Hagere Ertra)

CAPITAL
Asmara

GOVERNMENT
National Assembly (legislative), State Council (executive), and judiciary headed by Supreme Court

ADMINISTRATIVE ZONES
Anseba, Central, Gash-Barka, Northern Red Sea, Southern, and Southern Red Sea

PORTS
Assab and Massawa

CURRENCY
Nakfa (nkfa)

GEOGRAPHICAL AREA
46,830 square miles (121,320 square km)

HIGHEST AND LOWEST POINTS
Amba Soira (9,885 feet or 3,013 m)
Kobar Sink (380 feet or 116 m below sea level)

MAJOR RIVERS
Anseba, Barka, Gash, and Tekeze

POPULATION
4,025,100 (2000 estimate)

LITERACY
20% of the adult population

WORKING LANGUAGES
Tigrinya and Arabic

ETHNIC GROUPS
Tigray, Tigre, Afar, Beja, Nara, Kunama, Bilen, Rashaida, and Saho

MAIN RELIGIONS
Islam, Orthodox Christianity, and Roman Catholicism

MAJOR TRADING PARTNERS
Ethiopia, Saudi Arabia, and Italy

PRINCIPAL EXPORTS
Livestock, sorghum, textiles, and foods

PRINCIPAL IMPORTS
Processed goods, machinery, and oil products

HEROES OF THE INDEPENDENCE WAR
Isaias Afwerki—first president of Eritrea and leader of the former EPLF
Hamid Idris Awate—rebel leader who started armed struggle in 1961

IMPORTANT ANNIVERSARIES
May 24—Liberation and Independence Day
June 20—Martyrs' Day
September 1—Start of Armed Struggle

GLOSSARY

aba'ke ("ah-BAH-kay")
An unfermented drink made from a lentil-like grain.

amba ("AHM-bah")
A small tableland with steep walls and a flat top.

berbere ("bear-BEAR")
A hot sauce made of red chilies.

bun ("BOON")
Strong Eritrean coffee.

chira wata ("CHEE-ruh WAH-tuh")
A musical instrument similar to the violin.

dadda
A ritual fight between the young men of neighboring villages for a bountiful harvest.

djellabia ("JEL-lah-bay-ah")
A loose, long-sleeved robe for men.

douma ("DOE-mah")
A very strong alcohol made by the Afar from the sap of palm trees.

fool ("FOOL")
A bean puree.

frittata ("FRI-ta-tah")
Scrambled eggs with onions and tomatoes.

injera ("in-JEHR-uh")
A bread made from teff, wheat, or sorghum.

kirar ("KEE-rahr")
A guitar-like instrument with five strings.

kitcha ("KIT-cher")
A very thin unleavened bread baked from wheat or barley.

mido ("MEE-doh")
A traditional wooden comb worn by Eritrean men in their hair.

mies ("MEES")
An alcoholic beverage made with honey and water.

quno ("KOO-noh")
A hairstyle in which the hair is plaited in fine strands close to the scalp and left loose from the nape.

sheleel ("SHO-leel")
A group dance in which women shake their long plaited hair vigorously across their faces.

yekeniely ("YUH-ke-nee-lih")
An expression of gratitude; literally means "May God keep you."

zigni ("ZIHG-nee")
A chicken or beef stew.

BIBLIOGRAPHY

Habte Sillasie, Zeray. *What Is Your Name: Book of Eritrean & Ethiopian Names*. New Jersey: Africa World Press Inc., 2000.

Iyob, Ararat. *Blankets of Sand: Poems of War and Exile*. New Jersey: Red Sea Press, 1999.

Pateman, Roy. *Eritrea: Even the Stones Are Burning*. New Jersey: Red Sea Press, 1998.

Pollera, Alberto. *The Native Peoples of Eritrea* (translated by Linda Lappin). New Jersey: Red Sea Press, 2000.

INDEX

INDEX

INDEX

PICTURE CREDITS